HOW TO
LET GOD
MAKE
WHOOPEE

30 Days to Intimacy
WITH GOD

Dr. Joshua Williams

Copyright © 2018 Joshua C. Williams
All rights reserved.
ISBN-13: 9781728675244

Dedication

To my best friend on Earth, Tammy.

Acknowledgements

To my therapist, Kate Goodell: I wouldn't be here without you. Sessions with you are like watching Michael Jordan play basketball; you're doing what you were born to do, and you're the best at it.

To my lovely daughter, Natalie: You inspire me more than you could ever know. I love you to the moon and back!

To My mom and Dad: Thanks for letting me tell the world our stories. I love you both immensely.

To Paul and Perrianne Brownback: You got this all started. You told me I should write a book, and thirty days later, it was done! Thank you so much!

Day 1

"Now there is in Jerusalem by the sheep gate a pool, which is called in Hebrew Bethesda, having five porticoes. In these lay a multitude of those who were sick, blind, lame, and withered, waiting for the moving of the waters; for an angel of the Lord went down at certain seasons into the pool and stirred up the water; whoever then first, after the stirring up of the water, stepped in was made well from whatever disease with which he was afflicted. A man was there who had been ill for thirty-eight years. When Jesus saw him lying there, and knew that he had already been a long time in that condition, He *said to him, "Do you wish to get well?" The sick man answered Him, "Sir, I have no man to put me into the pool when the water is stirred up, but while I am coming, another steps down before me." Jesus *said to him, "Get up, pick up your pallet and walk." Immediately the man became well, and picked up his pallet and began to walk. - John 5:2-9 (NASB)

Ever wonder why God sent an angel down to stir the waters in John chapter 5? Sounds almost cruel. A multitude lay sick and dying around the pool of Bethesda. Yet only the first one in got healed. I can just picture God talking with Jesus and the Holy Spirit. "Hey fellas, wanna have some fun on this Saturday night? Let's send an angel down to stir the pool where all these crippled folk are (chuckling). Only the first one in will get healed. O man, that oughta make 'em squirm with desperation! Let's take bets on who gets there first. My money is on the guy with no legs. At least his arms are pretty strong."

Now, obviously that borders on disrespect. Nobody thinks

God was actually doing that. But why stir the pool to heal only one? He knew that every poor sick person within eyeshot would scurry as fast as he could when they saw the water stirred. And all but one would be severely disappointed.

Principal: Sometimes it's more important to get you moving than it is to instantly take away your problems.

This devotional is for everyone, but it will have greater resonance with those who have grown up in church. I don't mean to imply that every single church has failed in teaching us about relationship with God. I do, however, wish to state that in my experience, and according to the experiences of many people I know, not only has there been a void of practical teaching on the subject, but many of the things we were taught are just plain wrong or wildly ineffective. Like playing golf for years and then deciding to get proper lessons on technique, I've had to go through the painful yet transformative process of unlearning things. Maybe you can identify.

This is not a book meant to widely establish doctrine or theology. Of course, it is full of both. The aim of this devotional is practical application. Besides, I don't believe God created relationship to serve doctrine. The doctrine and theology are meant to serve the ultimate goal of relationship.

I've purposed to present this testimony and teaching in small chapters so it can read like a devotional. I've used bold, italics, and underlining to emphasize key principals, truths, and applications. Sometimes I chase a few rabbit trails, but that's not bad if you catch the rabbit, right? A rabbit makes a fine meal. Maybe even a hat or warm sock. My hope is for you to receive truths and principles which you can actually put to use. But many of these things will just transform you by the light of revelation. Some principles in this book are meant to challenge and stir you. And thus, you may have to grapple with some things on your own. All healthy outcomes.

Over the next 27 days, you might read things that make you angry. Or defensive. You may not feel it helps at all. But at the very least, I hope it gets you moving. Many of the messages in these pages emphasize truths on the opposite side of that coin: resting, waiting, being still, etc. However, if you're seemingly paralyzed and blind, sometimes you need to get motivated to move. As you will hear in Day 3, I was in a desperate state about my time with Lord. But I had to get motivated to change. I had to get stirred up to finally stop and do nothing.

I encourage you to read this over 30 days.

There is a lot of content. It will challenge you. Take time to absorb.

What did Jesus say to the crippled man when he came on the scene in John 5? "Do you wish to get well?"

Thirty-eight years. Thirty-eight years of someone beating him to the pool. Thirty-eight years among a bunch of sick, depressed, defeated, nasty people. Thirty-eight years of disappointment. If anyone but Jesus had asked him that question, his answer would've been, "WHAT THE *bleep* DO YOU THINK? Of course, I want to get well!"

The passage records that Jesus knew he'd been a long time in that state. "There's nobody to put me in. Someone always beats me there," the crippled man said.

"So quit doing the insanity of trying the same thing over and over. Do the opposite. Get up! Walk!" said Jesus in the gospel according to Josh. "What have you got to lose?"

I ask you, readers of this book, do you wish to get well? Been a long time in your frustrated state?

Do the opposite. Get motivated for something different than you're doing, and quite possibly different than you've been taught.

What have you got to lose?

Day 2

"Turning to his servants, the father said, 'Quick, bring me the best robe, my very own robe, and I will place it on his shoulders. Bring the ring, the seal of sonship, and I will put it on his finger. And bring out the best shoes you can find for my son. Let's prepare a great feast and celebrate. For this beloved son of mine was once dead, but now he's alive again. Once he was lost, but now he is found!' And everyone celebrated with overflowing joy.
"Now, the older son was out working in the field when his brother returned, and as he approached the house he heard the music of celebration and dancing."
- Luke 15:22-25 (TPT)

When I was in high school, my parents became pastors of a small church in Holdenville, Oklahoma. Mom and Dad took turns preaching. Mom was a traveling Pentecostal evangelist before she met my dad, so she knew how to "preach the anointin' down!" Yes, I said 'anointin'! She was a wonderful preacher!

One Sunday, she was preaching on the story of the prodigal son. She could get fairly animated, which we all loved. She asked the audience, "When the younger son came home, what did the father do? Did he say, 'Get away from me!'? Of course not!" She raised her voice and waved her hands to emphasize the point. "The father said, 'WHOOPEE! We're gonna make WHOOPEE tonight!'"

I don't think Mom knew that "make whoopee" has a sexual connotation. I think she meant to say, 'make merry'. Anyway, her version might well be accurate.

Nothing wrong with makin' a little whoopee when you're happy. Still, it gave my brothers and me one of our biggest laughs EVER!

WHOOPEE - boisterous convivial fun: **_merrymaking_** — *usually used with make*

-Merriam-Webster

God wants to 'make whoopee' over you. The challenge for us, as you'll see through this devotional, is to let Him.

While I'm using the term 'make whoopee' to illustrate the Father celebrating his son's return (and draw attention in the form of humor), I'm not totally separating it from an intimate connotation.

Do you know *why* God put us here? It wasn't because He needed more glory. And it wasn't because He wanted more servants.

Principle: You were made for intimacy.

Think back to the Garden of Eden. God created everything and called it good. Yet creation was still incomplete. Got had not created a helper suitable for man. So He caused a deep sleep to come upon Adam. He took a rib from Adam and made woman. We know the story well. Now why did God wait to create woman? Why didn't He create woman from the beginning?

God, being the master storyteller that He is, was painting a picture. He was telling the story of Himself. It wasn't good for man to be alone because it wasn't good for God to be alone. You see, He didn't create a woman and then decide to create marriage. He created both in one sweeping act. He did this because marriage is what he had intended all along. It symbolized the most intimate relationship on earth: The relationship God was to have with man.

Truth: Marriage is a type and shadow of our relationship with God.

Woman was not created to be alone. She was not created so that the man could have someone to procreate with. She was created to be his wife. With the creation of woman, God set up the most powerful and sacred relationship that humans can have: stating from the beginning man would leave his father and mother and cleave unto his wife, and they would become one flesh.

It's so important for us to know why God put us here. Many people think God put man here simply because He wanted to be glorified. And although there is truth in that, it wasn't the sole reason. God didn't put us here because He wanted someone to serve Him.

"For this is how much God loved the world—He gave His one and only, unique Son as a gift. So now everyone who believes in Him will never perish but experience everlasting life."
- John 3:16 (TPT)

"This is eternal life, that they may know You, the only true God, and Jesus Christ whom You have sent."
- John 17:3 (NASB)

He put us here to *know* Him. He put us here for relationship.

"You're blessed when you're at the end of your rope. With less of you there is more of God and his rule."
- Matthew 5:3 (MSG)

I'd had it.

I didn't necessarily blame God, but I was frustrated with any attempt to spend time with Him. It was quite awful. I looked at my life and saw no difference between myself and a "lost" person, other than the fact I believed I would go to heaven if I died, and the fact that I lived by a higher moral code than most. Still, regarding power, I was besieged with the same struggles, the same failed attempts to master "sin," the same conflict with people, the same anxieties, and the same check-to-check income that barely covered (or sometimes didn't cover) the bills. But there was something even worse. My "devotion" time was hard and void of experiencing the Lord.

It wasn't without trying on my part. I had been taught to "press-in," as it was called. It's an illustration taken from the woman with the issue of blood who pressed through the crowd to grab the hem of Jesus' garment. While there is truth in pressing in by faith to grab onto the promises of God, I found this is not the way to let God spend time with me.

But I didn't know I was supposed to let God spend time with me. I was trying to press-in. I was taught that He is the rewarder of those who diligently seek Him (Heb. 11:6).
 Again, there is truth in that passage as it applies to faith.

A man I once knew made a wise statement. It has continually brought great revelation in my life. He said, "Most people get off into error when they over-emphasize a truth." It happens all the time: Over-emphasis or misplaced truth. People grasp principles and apply them in the wrong instances.

In the same way, I was not applying principles and truths correctly.

Oh, but it wasn't for lack of trying. Most people who really know me can confirm that I would spend hours "seeking" the Lord and reading my Bible. But most of that time was filled with anxious striving and seeming fruitless practices.

I don't want to scare away any potential readers from a more conservative theological belief system. But I feel it is important to note that I spent hours praying in tongues. Yes, many, many hours. While I have enjoyed GREAT benefit from praying in the Spirit throughout my life, it did not help my problems in the area of time spent with the Lord.

I was smart enough to know the problem had to be on my end. I just couldn't seem to find any answers. King David said that if he had one wish, he'd rather be in the house of Lord all his days (Psalm 27). The Sons of Korah in Psalm 84 wrote the passage we sing so often, "Better is one day in Your courts than a thousand elsewhere." Peter wrote that we are rejoicing with a joy unspeakable and full of glory. This certainly was not my experience.

Don't get me wrong. I had times of "visitations" of the Lord's Presence. I enjoyed worshiping Him and being in a church service. But those visitations were inconsistent at best. And I had come to the end of my rope. I was depleted. The fact that I had become a middle school principal didn't help. It's a job filled with conflict. Learning to deal with conflict and overcome anxiety is another book for another time, but it certainly exacerbated my frustrations of trying to spend time with the Lord.

Most people I sought counsel from either shared the same frustrations, or barked at me that I wasn't "pressing-in" and believing enough.

So, I had an honest conversation with the Lord. It wasn't a true conversation, though. It was *me telling Him* something. I said, "Lord, I'm frustrated, but I'm not mad. I'm just done. Spending time seeking You is doing me no good. I still want to go to heaven. I don't plan to run off into a life of sin. I'm just not going to waste my time with any more devotions. But here's what I'll do. I'll give it thirty days. I'll get up early and wait on You for an hour or two every day for a month. If you don't show up, no hard feelings, but no more devotions for me. It's too frustrating and it's worthless."

Now you must understand something. For me to go to "spend time with the Lord" or "have quiet time" or "seek God" or "keep the morning watch" (or other endless Christianism's we use to label our duty to daily walk with the Lord) was an intense and lively activity. Me sitting quietly in a room for an hour was like a dereliction of duty. I was supposed to be SEEKING, for crying out loud! After all, that's who God rewards.

But that's exactly what I did. I got up early and drove to the middle school where I served as principal.

The morning sky was still black and filled with stars. It was as though I could feel the quiet of the world yet unawakened from peaceful slumber. I tried to make as little noise as possible as I cut through the back door of a portable building that served as our middle school office. The whole middle school had moved into portables when the school experienced an unexpected growth spurt shortly after moving to a brand-new campus. I liked that the middle school was detached from the rest of the school. It served my purpose well. I was seeking a place that would be undisturbed for a while.

I chose the computer lab because I figured it would be insulated from those crazy teachers who arrive at an ungodly hour, no pun intended. No one would happen in there for any reason at 5 a.m. in the morning.

Unlocking the heavy metal door, I let my body shield it from slamming closed behind me, so as not to send any ripples across the still morning air. All our portables were well used, brought over from the old campus. Rich in the blood, sweat, and tears of those who paved the way in the school's small beginnings, I could still sense the atmosphere of the old campus, and the faithfulness and prayers of sacrificial teachers, underpaid and overworked. The room smelled like school: construction paper and Expo marker mixed with a little student odor masked slightly with disinfectant.

I eased into a seat in the middle of the room and sat quietly. I didn't speak. I didn't worship. I just sat. For the next two hours, I listened to a computer in need of maintenance go in and out of sleep mode.

Nothing.

The next morning it was the same. Same dark night. Same old, historical portable. Same deafening quiet.

By the third morning, I was actually enjoying the peacefulness. At the very least, I was not worn out after spending time in a devotion, although it seems weird to even call it that. It was in the middle of this third morning I began to sense something: A peace entering the room. Although I'm now sure peace was there all along, I was just beginning to sense it. Scriptures began to come to mind, and a light of revelation was coming in these scriptures.

God led me to Psalm 23. This was to be a roadmap for letting Him spend time with me.

It didn't happen all at once. It was slow. Like little raindrops. But it was the beginning of a mind transformation. It absolutely changed how I now spend time with the Lord. In my frustration, I was actually lining up with what I was supposed to do according to scripture and according to God's design of relationship with Him. Over the next days and weeks, He revealed three secrets to me. They are not secrets of how to spend time with God. They are secrets of how to let God spend time with us.

Day 4

Two outfielders running for the same fly ball. Three actors who each think they're the lead in the play. The bass player and the drummer sparring to set the rhythm of the song. That coworker who thinks he's the boss in your supervisor's absence.

Not playing your role can cause frustration and pain in relationships. When you blur the lines of your role, it even makes people avoid you.

Micromanaging. Back-seat driving. Mother-in-lawing. God does none of these. He does His job, not yours. It's because He is a gentleman.

The Bible is the source of knowing our role. And the first place the Lord led me in the quiet of the middle school computer lab was Psalm 23.

Principle: Psalm 23 is a roadmap for letting God have relationship with you.

As we start down this journey together, begin to meditate on Psalm 23. Memorization of scripture can be a very effective tool. However, if you're like me, sometimes memorized scripture becomes just a rhythmic tape with someone else's spin on it, or a truth seen through a Christianese veil. Psalm 23 has been quoted so many times. For me, the meaning got lost in the method and rhythm. I challenge you to think of Psalm 23 as a pattern of letting God spend time with you.

Many scholars believe King David composed Psalm 23 at

the lowest point in his life.

King David had to flee Jerusalem, because his son Absalom tried to overthrow him. He was older at this time, and he was feeling the wear of a life of war and struggle. This betrayal is believed to be his lowest point. And many scholars think it's when he composed Psalm 23.

I disagree slightly. I believe this low point led David to get the revelation that led him to write Psalm 23. It's more than poetry and nice imagery. It's a divine revelation of how to spend time with God.

The first few verses of Psalm 23 are the foundation for the first secret the Lord revealed to me. It is the most important, because the other two secrets build on its foundation.

Principle: The beginning of a healthy relationship is knowing your role.

You cannot have a healthy relationship with anyone if you don't play your part. That's right, 'play your part'. I'm not going to say 'do' your part. It implies earning, and that's the opposite of what I'm talking about.

It's even worse if you are playing the other person's part. My Head of School, Mark Earwood, refers to a form of this as "not staying in your lane." I'm fairly sure that's a track and field analogy. Bad things happen when you get in another runner's lane.

Christians try yo do God's job for Him all the time. It frustrates the relationship. Can you imagine going into your boss's office, sitting down at his chair, barking orders to his secretary (sorry, administrative assistant), and making decisions on his behalf? That would quickly frustrate the relationship. It sends chills up my spine to even think of doing that. Most everyone would agree.

Still, we do this to God all the time. Why? We're taught to. The church has taught us to. And it makes us feel like we're being good Christians.

Principle: The grace of God, which is His power through relationship to transform you into Christ's image, is given to you when you walk in your role.

Peter and James both tell us that God resists the proud but gives grace to the humble (1 Peter 5 and James 4). We can get the picture of 'pride' as someone walking around like a rooster with his chest pooched out, or maybe someone who is full of himself. But pride can be much subtler and even preached as acceptable from church pulpits. As you'll see in the coming pages, we're often taught to do things that are really God's job. The practical application of being 'humble' is walking in our role.

Still wonder why your relationship with God isn't what it should be? It could be because you're resisting Him by playing His role. Chances are, you don't even realize you're doing it.

SECRET #1

INTIMATE FRIENDS KNOW THEIR OWN ROLES

"The Lord is my Shepherd..."

The beginning of the road to a healthy, experiential relationship with God is the revelation that "The Lord is my Shepherd..." When we realize this truth, like David, we'll confess, "'I shall not want.' I don't need anything else. I don't need to do anything else."

IT'S GOD'S JOB TO SHEPHERD HIS SHEEP

As I have alluded to already, one of the first things the Lord showed me in that little computer lab was that Psalm 23 is a roadmap for time with the Lord.

"The Lord is my Shepherd..." - Psalm 23:1.

So, let me ask you, do the sheep lead the shepherd? Do they come tell Him where to find pasture? Of course not. It's no different in time spent with the Lord.

Principle: The Shepherd leads your intimate times with Him.

"I will instruct you and teach you in the way which you should go; I will counsel you with My eye upon you."
- Psalms 32:8 (NASB)

Whatever you may call it: devotion, quiet time, time with the Lord, etc. HE is in charge, so let HIM lead. If you start DOING a bunch of stuff, you are doing HIS job. And He is a gentleman, so He'll let you. But it will be frustrating because you are not playing your part. You won't be experiencing Him any more than a person would enjoy a meal if they got up, pushed the cook and waiter out of the room, and started cooking and serving. This is perfectly illustrated in the story of Mary and her sister, Martha. One sister did her part. She experienced God. But the common wisdom of the time said Martha was the one filling the proper role. Not so.

He is our Shepherd. I knew this. I knew it in my head, anyway. Somehow, it wasn't translating into my time spent with Him. I had to *seek* Him, right? I had to press in. I had to seek him with all my heart!

That's not what sheep do, though.

Principle: The Shepherd seeks the sheep.

The Shepherd seeks the sheep, not the other way around. Somehow, I thought this principle of the shepherd seeking the sheep was only regarding salvation. After salvation, I was supposed to seek Him. And there was a picture in my mind of Him on His throne, waiting for me to approach.

Is that the picture you have? God on His throne, waiting for you to seek Him?

God is actually the Shepherd who is pursuing His sheep. Those are the roles we are to play, if you'll forgive me for saying it that way. If you're not careful, your 'seeking' can slide over into doing the Shepherd's job.

Sound too simple? It's easier to resist His leading than we might think.

It's amazing how many Christians don't know the Lord is our Shepherd. Lies and religion have blinded them just enough. They know God leads. But knowing God as leader doesn't result in the blissful confession: 'I shall not want'. We must have the revelation that He is our Shepherd.

Principle: The Shepherd leads with His voice.

"My sheep hear My voice, and I know them, and they follow Me…" - John 10:27 (NASB)

"For the Lord gives wisdom; From His mouth come knowledge and understanding." - Proverbs 2:6

"Your ears will hear a word behind you, 'This is the way, walk in it,' whenever you turn to the right or to the left." - Isaiah 30:21

Truth: Father God is not out in front of you. He is right beside you.

"I will instruct you (literally 'give you success') *and teach you* (literally to 'show you by pointing with my finger') *in the way which you should go; I will counsel you* (literally 'consult and provide for you') *with My eye upon you."- Psalms 32:8 (NASB)*

Think of this: the Shepherd is not leading from out in front of you. If He were out in front of you, he couldn't very easily be pointing to where you should go and have His eye on you. There's one position suited for this: HE IS RIGHT BESIDE YOU! His arm is around you. His eye is next to your eye. His cheek is next to your cheek. And He is pointing where to go.

"Do not be as the horse or as the mule which have no understanding, whose trappings include bit and bridle to hold them in check, Otherwise, they will not come near to you." - Psalms 32:9 (NASB)

This verse makes it very clear that the Shepherd doesn't want to be out in front of you, pulling you along. He doesn't want to control you by force!

"Hold on, Josh! You just messed up! You quoted Isaiah earlier. It said the voice of God comes from behind us. God can't be beside us if His voice came from behind!"

Yes! You are correct that the voice is behind us! But what happened just a little bit before that?

We turned.

Isaiah said we'd hear a voice behind us if we turned to the right or left. Why? BECAUSE THE SHEPHERD WAS BESIDE US! We left Him behind when we turned. But He lovingly calls to us. Why?

Because He leads with His VOICE!

The Shepherd seeks you. And if you'll let Him, He'll come along side you and put his arm around you. He'll put His cheek next to yours, stretch out his arm, point ahead and say, "This is the way! Walk in it!"

The practical application is simply this: trust the Lord to lead in your devotion time. Don't feel the obligation to 'do' a lot of things. You'll be amazed at the difference.

Day 6

"The Lord is my Shepherd..."

"I will instruct you and teach you in the way which you should go; I will counsel you with My eye upon you."
- Psalms 32:8 (NASB)

IT'S OUR JOB TO SEE GOD AS OUR SHEPHERD AND TRUST THAT HIS NATURE IS GOOD

It's so important to know the nature of your Shepherd. Why? Because you must trust in His goodness. He is good and He leads us lovingly. And His *"goodness and lovingkindness shall follow* (you) ALL *the days of* (your) *life."*
- Psalm 23:6

So many good people that think God leads by the bridle of circumstances. "God closed this door," they say. "Maybe He'll open a window somewhere."

Ever had a closed door? Ever stop to consider that the Shepherd may be pointing you to knock on the closed door?

Bob Goff, author of New York Times best-seller *Love Does*, says it this way: *"I used to think God guided us by opening and closing doors, but now I know sometimes God wants us to kick some doors down."*

Principle: The Shepherd doesn't wish to lead by bridling you through a circumstance.

It's clear according to Psalm. 32:9 that the Lord doesn't desire to lead by bridling us. I don't believe God ever leads us by circumstances. If He does, it's a very low level of relationship. We have to be careful that we're not looking to fate or omens. It's so easy to do. We think because something didn't work out, it must have been the Shepherd's will that it didn't. However, there is a sure way to know. The Shepherd gives you success by pointing, while advising you with His arm around you, and His eye right next to yours. It's hard to mistake this.

Principle: There is a difference in the favor of the Lord going before you and circumstances being against you.

I'll share a story in a later chapter about how Tammy and I met our therapist at a friend's wedding. I believe it was totally arranged by the Lord. I believe He connected us to her. Similarly, when Tammy and I moved to Texas from Oklahoma completely by faith, we had no jobs. A friend, in the church we started attending, put our resumes in the hands of her principal at a private school. One thing led to another, and I started teaching at Liberty Christian School and soon became an administrator.

Tammy and I often look back and wonder how significant those two stories are. Relationships with certain people are what connected us with other people, and that's quite amazing. So, what would've happened if I hadn't attended that wedding? What would've happened if our friend from church hadn't given my resume to her principal? The favor of the Lord would have prospered us anyway.

You see, the favor of the Lord leading you is entirely different than being bridled by circumstances. When I was at Liberty Christian School, I had a year that was particularly rough. We found out in May that Natalie, our daughter, had Crohn's disease. It felt as if the rug had been pulled out from under us. The news of our daughter having a disease was overwhelming. A few days later, I was at work trying to wrap up the year.

In the middle of my end-of-the-year evaluation, Tammy called. She was clearly upset.

"I can't breathe! I feel like I'm having a panic attack," she exclaimed.

I hurriedly excused myself, jumped in the car, and drove toward home as quickly as I could. Traffic was bad, so I chose an alternate route that led me through a little community who had a very diligent policeman. Keeping within the confines of the speed laws was not on the forefront of my mind.

Of course, the diligent, little policeman pulled me over. I tried explaining the situation to him. He seemed unphased and even moved at a snail's pace. I got the slowest issued ticket in history. A whopping $230 one!!

When I finally made it home, Tammy seemed to be doing better. I prayed with her. We decided not to go to the hospital at that time.

In my rush to get to Tammy, I had quickly pulled into the driveway and left all my things in the car. So I walked back out through the garage to retrieve them. As I did, I noticed our cat laying by the backyard gate. She was laying upside down. I thought, "Silly cat! How did you get out again?" I was in no mood for playing. Anytime we even cracked the back door, she would bolt outside, and play the most annoying game of "Run from the humans who are trying to get you back indoors."

I was in no mood for games.

As I walked closer to her, I realized, tragically, that she was not playing a game. Oh, how I wish she were! Yep, I had run her over in my frantic arrival. She was still alive, but barely.

Without going into detail, there was no way to save her life, and I mercifully had to put her down.

This cat was Natalie's love. She named her Joy. Joy slept with Natalie every night! And they adored each other.

Bad day, huh? We've all had them. It felt like the whole world was against me. In that moment, it's tempting to believe that somehow God is either orchestrating this, or He is ALLOWING this for some purpose.

But, THIS IS NOT HOW THE LORD LEADS US! These weren't signs from heaven. These were circumstances of life that happen. However, I believe someone was manipulating many of these things. And it wasn't God! It was our adversary, the devil. He's the one that Peter tells us to be sober and vigilant about. He's the one we are to armor-up against.

I understand how it feels in the moment when hard times come. We feel so out of control. So many times, I've heard Christians who've had a similar type day blame God. They say He must've had some purpose in it, although they're not sure what the purpose was. But if you think this is God's nature, it will hinder you in letting Him spend time with you.

.

Day 7

"The Lord is my Shepherd..."

Some Christians even go as far as to say God is the author of bigger tragedies, like someone dying or contracting a disease. Many even believe God causes natural disasters or severe traffic injuries.

My earthly father was and is a good man. But he wasn't perfect. In fact, much of the work I've had to do in therapy is because of my dad's unhealthiness. I don't say this to disparage him in any way. I say this so that you, the readers, can trust that I have empathy with those who've endured father problems. He did the best he could with what he knew.

Still, my dad never hid behind a tree and threw rocks at me. He never hid around a corner and threw a barrier in the way so I'd go a different direction. Isn't Father God more 'good' than our earthly fathers? Why would we think *He* leads in this manner?

My father never ran me over with a car to teach me not to walk in the street. I hear Christians blaming Father God for things like this all the time. Let me just say, if God is leading you this way, it is a VERY LOW LEVEL of relationship.

Someone might say, "Yeah, Josh, but God isn't here in physical form like my earthly dad was. He has to use various signs, and even problems, to lead us or otherwise we won't hear Him"

I would like to challenge you to search the scriptures and see if they reveal God's nature in this manner. In day 5, I talked about how God leads by His voice, and counsels us with His eye on us.

When I was a kid, my earthly dad often believed I was not listening fully to him. About 99.9% of the time, he was correct. He'd have to tell me something several times. Often, he'd grab my chin and speak slowly and deliberately in my face.

But he NEVER poked a hole in my car tire, put cancer on me, or made me have a car accident.

"Yeah, Josh, but I'm not sure I'd hear Him if he spoke. Sometimes I need Him to show me a sign or open a door."

That's pretty low-level communication for the God Who lives on the inside of you. Another important point: when you dabble in the realm of signs and doors, your messing in an area the devil himself can manipulate. The devil can sometimes close doors. He can manufacture signs.

I'm not saying God won't cause things to turn around for good. I've heard people testify that a loved one died, and at the funeral, several people received the gift of salvation and became born again. They connect the dots that God must've caused the loved one to die so those people would get saved. However, that's not what the Bible teaches. Just because Father God turned it around for good doesn't mean He caused it.

Principle: People in need of answers and comfort often feel a sense of peace that God must've been in control of the bad things that happened to them. But this comfort will be short-lived and will have long term repercussions for relationship with God.

As I already alluded to earlier, my Natalie became very sick a few years ago. We couldn't figure out what was wrong. By the end of her 5th grade year, she looked like someone who hadn't eaten in weeks. She was slowly dying of malnutrition. We finally received a correct diagnosis of Crohn's disease. And it devastated us.

In cases like this, it brings some answers to the 'why' to say things like, "Well, God is in control." We want to feel that there's meaning in what is happening. We want to feel like God is with us. We don't want to explore the repercussions of "What if this were the devil?"

My circumstances may be different than yours, but I understand what it's like to be frozen with fear and ravaged with loss. I've lost three of my best friends to tragedy: two to sickness and one to a swimming accident. I've lost students to car wrecks. Inevitably, someone in the middle of the situation will say, "It was God's time for them to go."

I even heard one person say, "The fact that she died instantly proves it was her time to go." I don't get as worked up as I once did over statements like this. I realize people are seeking comfort through meaning and control. I've been there. Still, I have to ask the question: How did you connect the dots? How did you get instant death as proof it was God's will?

Principle: God allowing something, doesn't mean He willed it.

"Ok Josh, but God can control everything, right? So, He at least allowed those bad things to happen." True, He *CAN*. But how do you connect the dots that if He allowed it, He must have desired it to happen? The truth is, God doesn't control everything.

Truth: God isn't controlling everything. He isn't

controlling you. He also isn't controlling the things He's given to your authority.

I know that is hard for some people to swallow. But remember, He plays HIS role. If He were controlling you, He wouldn't be playing His part. If He were taking charge of things He gave to you, He'd be playing YOUR role. And God doesn't do that.

And, yes, He will allow you to make mistakes, even if it means collateral damage.

Why? He knows how to live in relationship. Therefore, He abides by Secret #1.

So not everything that happens is God's will or desire. God will *allow* a lot of things! He'll let you fall off a roof and break your leg if you don't have the sense to use a safety harness. It doesn't mean He wanted that to happen. It just means He won't invade your role.

"But Josh, can't God save me if I fall off that roof? Can't he send His angels to keep me in all my ways and bear me up if I stumble?"

Yes! Absolutely. But you have to ask Him to! He won't come into your role without an invitation.

Just a quick point about prayer, which can probably be further developed into another book another time, but it's worth noting here. Christians misunderstand prayer. Many Christians would pray, "Lord, if it be thy will, save me from falling off this roof." Let me clear this up: It IS His will to save you from falling off the roof! That's not the question. The question has to do with YOUR will. Are you going to ask? Are you going to invite Him?

Why is this so important? Because it goes to the nature of God. You don't believe He is your Shepherd if you think He goes around bridling people through circumstances. If you think He will put cancer on you, or kill your friend in a car wreck because it's their time, what do you think He'll do in your devotion time? How can you trust He'll be good?

I don't claim to have an answer for everything you may have endured. I don't have answers for why my friends died at such young ages. It hurts and I don't mean to speak carelessly about anyone's tragedy. I do, however, have a clear answer for the nature of God: He is good and He plays His role.

I have heard people testify that God 'shut up the heavens' and didn't speak to them. Really? God ignored you? To teach you some lesson? The bible teaches the opposite.

Principle: If you think God holds back from speaking to you or giving you what you need, you won't receive ANYTHING from Him.

James makes this very plain:

"But if any of you lacks wisdom, let him ask of God, who **GIVES TO ALL GENEROUSLY AND WITHOUT REPROACH** (He's not picking you apart), and it will be given to him. But he must ask in faith without any doubting, for the one who doubts is like the surf of the sea, driven and tossed by the wind. For that man ought not to expect that he will receive anything from the Lord, *being* a double-minded man, unstable in all his ways. - James 1:8

You won't receive from God if you don't believe He is the good Shepherd.

"Yeah, Josh, but we are just supposed to trust Him

sometimes, even when we don't know why things happen." True. But He is not asking you to trust in His seeming randomness.

Truth: God is not expecting you to trust in His sovereignty. He invites you to trust in His GOODNESS!

So many Christians go around trusting in the sovereignty of God. And thus, they are living a life of "what will be will be". They don't experience His goodness, because to them, His goodness is comprised of random, sovereign acts that God does for some higher purpose than He can reveal. The truth is, God IS sovereign. HE IS SOVEREIGNLY GOOD!

And He sovereignly plays His role.

"I shall not want..."

IT'S GOD'S JOB TO GIVE YOU WHAT YOU NEED, AND EVEN WHAT YOU WANT.

As I already stated, when we come to the realization and revelation that HE is truly our Shepherd, like David, we'll confess 'I shall not want!' This is more than a head nod to a truth. It's an empowering "ah-ha" revelation. It's a place of complete confidence that we'll never lack. Worry ceases when we rest in the fact that he will truly "...*give you the desires your heart.*" - Psalm 37:4

IT'S OUR JOB TO EXPECT.

Expectancy is a natural outcome of arriving at the place 'I shall not want.'

Principle: 'Waiting' in the Bible has much more to do with anticipating and expecting than 'doing' nothing.

Trains. Grocery lines. Traffic. Department of motor vehicles. Commercials. Slow internet speed. Need I say more?

We don't like to wait. Time is valuable. Formerly, when I came across scriptures about 'waiting' on the Lord, I would immediately bristle. I would think, "So I'm just supposed to do nothing? And everything will just work out?"

"Yet those who wait for the Lord
Will gain new strength;

*They will mount up with wings like eagles,
They will run and not get tired,
They will walk and not become weary." - Isaiah 40:31*

"Wait for the Lord; Be strong and let your heart take courage; yes, wait for the Lord." - Psalm 27:14

Years ago, before my computer lab experience with the Lord, I was so frustrated about life. I'd talk to my mom on the phone, and she'd say, "Rest, honey. Rest in the Lord and wait for Him." It was very good advice.

But inside, I'd be thinking, "If you tell me to 'rest in the Lord' one more time, I'm going to reach through this phone and slap you!" I'm glad I didn't say it out loud. Mom was giving me the correct advice. But I think many of you can identify with my frustration.

Don't get me wrong. There is GREAT value in being still. There are times to quiet yourself and listen for the voice of the Lord. It would be hard to over-emphasize the importance of being still and listening.

But the truth is, 'wait' according to these scriptures has little to do with standing still and doing nothing. It is the Hebrew word 'qavah'. It means 'to bind or twist" and implies 'strength', as in reference to making a strong rope. Gesenius's Hebrew-Chaldee Lexicon also defines 'wait' in these scriptures as 'to expect'. The Blue Letter Bible defines 'wait' as 'to look eagerly for'.

When you realize that the Lord is your Shepherd, and you wrap yourself in that revelation and promise, you are 'twisting' yourself together with the Lord.

*"Do you not know? Have you not heard?
The Everlasting God, the Lord, the Creator of the ends of the*

*Earth,
Does not become weary or tired.
His understanding is inscrutable.
He gives strength to the weary,
And to him who lacks might He increases power."
- Isaiah 40:28-29*

He gives you strength! When you wrap yourself in that promise and fully expect it to happen, that's waiting. And those who 'wait' receive.

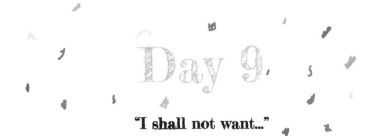

Day 9.

"I shall not want..."

Principle: 'Hope' in the Bible has much more to do with 'expecting' than 'wishing.'

Your friend has a loved one in serious condition at the hospital. You call or visit your friend and ask how his loved one is doing. "Is she going to make it?", you ask.

"Well, I sure hope so," he answers. "The prognosis isn't good."

'Hope' in this scenario is totally different from how the Bible uses it. In this instance, your friend is expressing a deep wish.

"Hey, Joe, did you get that job you interviewed for?"

"Gosh, I don't know yet. I sure hope so. The interview didn't go so well."

Joe in this scenario is wishing to get the job. And there is nothing wrong with that. But it's not Biblical hope. In both of these examples, there is an implied message that the 'wish' is probably unlikely to happen. This is how we tend to use the word 'hope'.

Romans 8:24-25 is a great example of Biblical 'hope', but it's not the only one. I encourage you to do further study on your own.

*"For in **hope** we have been saved, but **hope** that is seen is not **hope**; for who **hopes** for what he already sees? But if*

we **hope** for what we do not see, with perseverance we wait eagerly for it." - Romans 8:24-25

Vine's Expository Dictionary of New Testament Words defines 'hope' here as 'the happy anticipation of good.' Even without Vine's help, one can see that in the context of verse 25, there is a great expectancy. 'Hope' is not merely a good wish among dire circumstances.

*"Let Your lovingkindness, O Lord, be upon us, according as we have **hope**d in You." - Psalm 33:22*

I won't take time here to define 'lovingkindness', but it is a GREAT word to study. It is the greatest expression of love and favor from the Lord. We really don't even have a good English word for this Hebrew word. King David in Psalm 63 said it was better than life itself. Today, we'd probably say it's better than sex.

When do we receive this 'lovingkindness'? And to what degree? To the measure that we have the happy anticipation of it.

Principle: 'Seek' in the Bible has more to do with 'looking for an arrival' than 'searching for someone who is hiding.'

I never really liked playing hide and seek as a kid. It was fun half the time. Hiding was awesome. Seeking, not so much. I never was good at seeking people who really weren't wanting to be found.

I think the scriptures that encourage seeking the Lord made me feel like God was playing 'hide and seek'. He really wasn't wanting to be bothered. But if you actually did the work of finding Him hiding in the den where He could 'be away from the kids for a while', then He'd go ahead and reward you.

Again, that's not how the Bible defines 'seek'.

The Bible does paint a picture in the first few chapters of Proverbs of the benefit of seeking wisdom from the scriptures. Even in this case, it compares 'seeking' to a treasure hunt. Hidden treasure implies something hidden FOR YOU, not FROM YOU. It's a totally different feeling than the game of hide and seek.

In Day 5, I alluded to 'seeking' the Lord as something that is not our job. I'm not moving from that principle. In that case, seeking is pursuing, and it's God's job to pursue us. The Shepherd seeks the sheep (Luke 15). However, there is a 'seeking' which we are supposed to do.

Let's look at 'seeking' in the context of spending time in the Lord's Presence. One of my favorite passages is Psalm 63:

*O God, You are my God; I shall **seek** You earnestly;*
My soul thirsts for You, my flesh yearns for You,
In a dry and weary land where there is no water.
Thus, I have seen You in the sanctuary,
To see Your power and Your glory.
Because Your lovingkindness is better than life,
My lips will praise You.
So, I will bless You as long as I live;
I will lift up my hands in Your name.
My soul is satisfied as with marrow and fatness,
And my mouth offers praises with joyful lips.

Gesenius's Hebrew-Chaldee Lexicon says that the Hebrew word 'shachar' translated 'seek' means 'to break forth as light, as dawn." In this particular passage, it means 'to long after.' Blue Letter Bible defines 'seek' here as 'to look early' or 'to look diligently.'

So here is my interpretation of the Hebrew meaning: 'to seek' means that you long for it like longing to see the sunrise, so you wake up early to see it happen.

Did you make the sun rise? Of course not. But you can get up early and get in a place to see it. That's seeking. In reference to the Lord spending time with you, He comes every morning. The question is NOT will it happen. The question is will you get up and experience Him? In this case, HE is the rewarder (Hebrews 11:6) of you who got up early to look. He is not the rewarder of someone who through blood, sweat, and tears finally found Him hiding in the den.

"I shall not want..."

Over the last two days, we looked at the meaning of three words which are often misunderstood in reference to our relationship with God. Now let's put it all together with this very familiar passage we've all quoted and sang about:

This I recall to my mind,
*Therefore, I have **hope**.*
The Lord's lovingkindnesses indeed never cease,
For His compassions never fail.
They are new every morning;
Great is Your faithfulness.
"The Lord is my portion," says my soul,
*"Therefore, I have **hope** in Him."*
*The Lord is good to those who **wait** for Him,*
*To the person who **seeks** Him. - Lamentations 3:21-15*

So, at this point, I hope you can see, or at least start to see, some simple truths. As Jesus said in John 8:32, 'The truth will MAKE you free.' It doesn't say SET you free. "Setting you free" implies immediacy. "Making you free" implies a process. Mind transformation is definitely a process, but it doesn't have to be a long one.

Still, you may question, how? "Josh, how do I step into the reality of what you are explaining?"

You are going to hear me repeat some simple spiritual rules and practices, illustrating them in various ways. While they are truly simple, they are not always easy.

Principle: The way you walk out your faith is the same way

you received salvation.

How did you receive the gift of salvation and become born again? Did you work at it? Did you do anything to earn it?

No.

You confessed with your mouth the Lord Jesus and believed in your heart that God raised Him from the dead (Romans 10:9-10). That simple act allowed you to receive what is arguably the greatest miracle of all time: new birth. Two things are important: confessing and believing.

But there are two additional important things to remember. You receive the promises of the Bible by confessing it's truths. You can't confess just anything and receive it. The other important thing is faith isn't an act of your will. You can't just decide to have faith. Faith comes by hearing the Word according to Romans 10:13.

Principle: Faith is a fruit of the Spirit.

Love, joy, peace, patience, kindness, goodness, gentleness, faithfulness, and self-control. We learned this in Sunday School through a song or chant.

Faithfulness. I got to studying about this. I'm confused why it was translated "faithfulness." It doesn't mean faithfulness in the way we use the word. It means FAITH. The Greek word is *pistis*. It means stong belief or conviction. It's the same word Jesus used to describe the centurion who had a sick servant and asked Jesus to "speak the word only and my servant will be healed." It's the same word used to describe the faith of the woman who was healed by touching the hem of Jesus' garment. It is mountain-moving faith.

And guess what? IT IS A FRUIT!

You can't will yourself to have fruit. Fruit grows from relationship and intimacy. It grows from hearing the Word.

DON'T **_TRY_** TO BELIEVE!!!!! Let faith simply come. Trying to believe will negate the principle.

God told Joshua (Joshua 1:8) that HE (clarifying what is man's job) would make HIS way prosperous and have success by doing one thing: the book of the law wasn't to depart from his MOUTH, but he must MEDITAITE (means to 'mutter' or 'murmur') on it day and night.
God also told Joshua to "be strong and very courageous." Sound familiar? Does it sound like "to twist"? Those who "wait" (twist or be strong) on the Lord shall gain new strength.

Psalm 1:2-3

But his delight is in the law of the Lord,
And in His law he meditates day and night.
He will be like a tree firmly planted by streams of water,
Which yields its fruit in its season
And its leaf does not wither;
And in whatever he does, he prospers.

"Meditate" in this passage also means to "murmur or mutter".

Principle: *You receive or walk in biblical promises by confessing and believing.*

You receive by confessing and believing.
But you must confess the truth(s). And you must allow faith to be a fruit by meditating (muttering) on the scriptures.

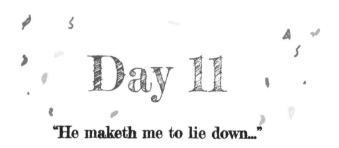

"He maketh me to lie down..."

The first thing the Lord begins to do when He comes to spend time with you, is put you in a position which allows Him to work. He wants you to take a resting position. Why? Because it restores correct relationship. He is much more interested getting relationship with Him in the right place than He is correcting any wrong behavior or attitude.

Why?

Because wrong behavior and wrong attitudes don't separate you from Him!

A wrong position does. God doesn't resist those with problems. He doesn't resist those who are in sin. Yes, you heard me correctly. He resists the PROUD! Grace is given to the humble. And being humble means playing your part!

IT'S GOD'S JOB TO GIVE YOU REST

I was appalled at the things the Lord began to show me in the quiet of the middle school computer lab. Firstly, I was appalled that I was receiving answers without having to do anything. It rocked my world! I was also appalled that I was seeing truths which were plain as day, but I'd just never seen them. I had diligently practiced reading the Bible on my own. I read it faithfully, but I'd been looking at it through the lens of others' teaching.

Principle: One of the first things the Lord will do when you allow Him to spend time with you is make you lie down.

According to Exodus 33, Moses pitched a tent (say that fast three times) way, way, way outside the camp. We'll talk about why it was far away later. Everyone who wanted to seek the Lord would go to this tent.

He called it the Tent of Meeting. Wow! Definitely antithetical to my experiences with seeking the Lord. What do you call your time with the Lord? Is it a meeting? My tent would be rightly called the Tent of Frustration or Tent of Striving.

Anyway, when Moses would go to the Tent of Meeting, every person would rise up and watch him. Then, after Moses entered the tent, the pillar of cloud would descend and stand at the door of the tent. Every person in Israel would fall down and worship. God would speak to Moses face to face, as a man speaks to a friend. Is that your prayer time is like? Do all your neighbors stand at their door and watch you go to your prayer closet? Does a pillar of cloud come down and stand at the door? Mine neither.

Then Moses said to the Lord, "See, You say to me, 'Bring up this people!' But You Yourself have not let me know whom You will send with me. Moreover, You have said, 'I have known you by name, and you have also found favor in My sight.' Now therefore, I pray You, if I have found favor in Your sight, let me know Your ways that I may know You, so that I may find favor in Your sight. Consider too, that this nation is Your people." And He said, "My presence shall go *with you*, and I will give you rest." Then he said to Him, "If Your presence does not go *with us*, do not lead us up from here. For how then can it be known that I have found favor in Your sight, I and Your people? Is it not by Your going with us, so that we, I and Your people, may be distinguished from all the *other* people who are upon the face of the earth?"
- Exodus 33:12-16

Moses was in the Presence of God, but he was not at rest. He asked God, "You've told me to bring up this people, but who are you going to send with me?" (My translation)

I love this! Moses was such a good pray-er. He was basically asking, "How do I stay in relationship with You?" He further asked, "Show me Your ways that I MAY KNOW YOU!"

So, God showed Moses how to walk in relationship. He basically said, "Play your role, Moses!"

Principle: If you don't let God make you lie down, you'll soon find yourself without His presence.

According to Exodus 33, God answered Moses, "My Presence shall go wth you, and I will give you rest." Why was God giving Moses rest? Because Moses was tired? No. Because it wasn't Moses job to carry those burdens. It was God's job. Moses had finally gotten to a place where he let God make him lay down.

Moses basically answered, "That's great. It's not even worth going if You don't go with us. It's not worth it without relationship. How else are we going to be any different than any other nation?" (Again, my translation)

Moses knew that it was all about relationship. Remember me back at the computer lab? In my frustration, I didn't realize I was praying Moses' prayer. I was basically saying, "None of this is really worth it without relationship. If Your Presence doesn't go with me, don't even send me up!"

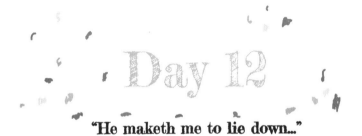

"He maketh me to lie down..."

IT'S OUR JOB TO COME AS WE ARE

"Come to Me, all who are weary and heavy-laden, and I will give you rest. Take My yoke upon you and learn from Me, for I am gentle and humble in heart, and you will find rest for your souls. For My yoke is easy and My burden is light."
- Matt. 11:28

Jesus wasn't offering to take the burdens of some weary folk for a while. He wasn't giving them a breather. He was beckoning them to let Him step into His proper role as they step into theirs.

But they had to come just as they were.

"Wait, Josh! Stop! That's what we do during the altar call of a Billy Graham crusade. It's how we respond on the fifth night of revival. It's how we finally give in on the last day of youth camp, when we've resisted the beckoning call to salvation but finally got scared enough by the suggestion we might die in a car wreck upon exiting the building (And go straight to hell, of course!). We don't come as we are AFTER salvation!"

Oh yes. This is a call to Christians. It is a lifestyle.

Principle: *You must learn to lay down.*

There's a place where Jesus gives us rest.
It's the place where we come with our burdens.
It's where He makes rest available.

"Come to me ALL who are weary and heavy-laden, and I will give you rest."

But there is a place where we FIND rest. "Take my yoke upon you and learn from me…and you will find rest for your souls." We have to be taught to lie down. It doesn't come naturally. The world teaches us to 'do' and to 'earn'. Unfortunately, the church teaches us the same thing. There is a process to letting God 'make' you lie down, just like the truth 'makes' you free.

Principle: You have to come to God with your unsettled emotions.

One truth I realized, in Exodus 33, was the emotional state of Moses when he spent time with God.

The crazy thing is that Moses was depressed! That's right, he was in the Presence of God with all that miraculous pomp and circumstance, and he was depressed. In Numbers 11, we see a more vivid description of Moses' interaction with God. While it is a separate occasion, he is still in the tent of meeting. Moses was so frustrated that he asked God to go ahead and kill him. That's right, he said, "God, if you're going to treat me this way, kill me now!"

Principle: God will still run to spend time with you when you're down, depressed, anxious, and frustrated.

None of those things keep God's Presence away. In fact, he is a VERY PRESENT help in times of trouble according to Psalm 46:1. How had I not seen this?

I had been taught that I was not walking in faith if down, depressed, frustrated, etc. And I certainly wasn't pleasing God, much less, in His Presence.

Jesus said, *"Come to me all who are weary and heavy-laden…"* (Matthew 11). One would think the Presence of God is exactly the place for the down and depressed.

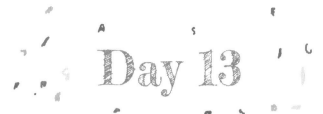

Day 13

"He leadeth me beside the still waters..."

IT'S GOD'S JOB TO BEAR ALL YOUR BURDENS

"...casting all your anxiety on Him, because HE CARES FOR YOU." - 1 Peter 5:7

"Cast your burden upon the Lord and He will sustain you." - Ps. 55:22

"Come to me, all you who are heavy-laden, and I will give you rest." - Matt. 11:28

In Psalm 23, the roadway for letting God spend time with you, the phrase "he leads me beside still waters" literally means He guides you to a restful watering place.

Principle: God doesn't bear your burdens because He's a nice guy. He does it because it's His job.

God is good. But He is more than just a nice guy.

We can bring our requests, burdens, or problems to the Lord, and we can have faith in His goodness. There's no question. However, we have access to something even more than His goodness.

My friend, Daniel, is a really nice guy. One of nicest guys I know. He would probably help me with anything I needed. But he has no obligation to help me. Even Daniel, at some point, might run out of goodness. If I asked him over and over and over to give me a ride home, or give me a lift somewhere, at some point, he'd probably say "no."

I know people who will watch my kids. I trust them and I pay for them to do so. It's goodness mixed with a little business. At some point, there are babysitting situations where my friends would even say "no" or "it's not enough money." They may never say it exactly like that, but they would feel that way.

I have a family relationship with my kids. It's biological. It's parental. It's a covenant. I 'babysit' them and drive them around. In my humanity, I get tired of doing so. But it's my job.

God is good. He's a 'good guy' if you will.

But it's His job to carry your burdens. You have a covenant relationship with Him. Your job is to take Jesus's burden, which is easy and light. He takes ALL of yours.

Matthew 11:28 says, "Come to me, all you who are heavy-laden, and I will give you rest…take my yoke upon you, for my yoke is easy and my burden is light."

1 Peter 5:7 says, "Casting ALL your care on Him, for He cares for you…"

This isn't just a nice offer like, "Oh, hey, I'll watch the kids for a while…" or "I see you're burdened, so let me give you a break since you're struggling with burdens you should be able to bear. Since you can't seem to, I'll give you a little relief. It's true everyone needs relief from time to time."

WRONG! It's not your job. More importantly, you weren't made to carry your burdens.

Principle: Like anything used for something outside of its purpose, you'll eventually experience a breakdown under burdens.

Ever used an adjustable wrench as a hammer? I have. Usually because I don't want to crawl out from under the car or down off the ladder to get the tool I need. My dad used to always say, "The tool you need for every job is always the one you forgot to bring."

An adjustable wrench will work for a while as a hammer, but eventually it will break down. It will even be broken to the point of not functioning in the role it was made for.

You can carry burdens for a while, but you weren't made to. Your emotions, your mind, and your body weren't made for anxiety and worry. Eventually, you'll break down. If you go too long under burdens, you'll not even be able to function in the roles God intended.

Cast your burdens on the Lord. It's His job to take them.

How?

Meditate on the scriptures that reveal Him as your burden-taker. Make an out-loud confession of the truth.

Here's an example:

"Lord, I'm worried about my daughter. But Psalm 55 says to cast my burdens on you and you will sustain me. It's not my job to worry about my daughter. I give it to You. I believe what Your Word says."

Wait. Expect results.

Day 14

"He leadeth me beside the still waters..."

IT'S OUR JOB TO CAST OUR BURDENS ON THE LORD

You won't experience God spending time with you if you are bearing your burdens. Why? Because you are doing HIS job when you bear your own burdens. That means you are walking in pride, and God is actually resisting you. You won't receive His grace. You won't experience His presence.

"OK Josh, I see it. But how do I do it?" you might ask. "How do I cast my burdens on the Lord?"

It's going to sound simple, but I realize simple doesn't always equal easy.

Principle: Much of the freedom will come in simply realizing it's not your job to bear your burdens.

Take time to meditate on the fact that ANY burden you feel AT ALL is GOD'S RESPONSIBILITY! Conflict, pain, hurt, stress, job situations, family situations, past situations, financial situations…all GOD'S to bear!

Next, start believing what the scriptures say.

Principle: Faith works in the same manner it did when you received salvation.

"Just as you received Christ Jesus as Lord, so walk ye in Him…" - Colossians 2:6

How did you receive Jesus? According to Romans 10:9-10, you confessed with your mouth and you believed in your heart.

How does faith come? By hearing the Word. Ever wonder why we have praise songs to start a church service? They are usually songs with simple lyrics, and they usually contain a lot of repetition. Why? Well, it's not random. THERE IS PURPOSE IN IT!

Most people who come into a church service aren't brimming with faith. The pressures of the week have beaten them up. They are empty. They come to church to get filled. If you start with a song that encourages them to declare simple truths like *"I'll sing because You are Good, I'll dance because You are good, I"ll shout because You are good, You are good to me!"*, after a while, their hearts will start to believe the truth their mouths are confessing. It's a spiritual principal. Faith arises, and they are in a much better place to receive the message.

"...faith cometh by hearing, and hearing the Word of God." - Romans 10:17

According to Mark 11:23-24, Jesus said once you get to the place in prayer where you believe what YOU SAY when you pray, you have it.

Principle: Feelings are fruit. Give them time. They don't grow overnight, but they'll start to!

"Ok, Josh. I've confessed. And I believe these truths. But I don't feel any different!"

You know what this means? It means you're human.

When you cast your burdens on the Lord, you WILL feel

some immediate release. But your feelings will take a little time to adjust. IT IS OK!

In the Word of Faith movement, we somehow got the notion that if our feelings didn't immediately line up, we weren't in faith. This is not true at all. It would be the same as saying, "I planted a watermelon seed this morning and nothing has grown!"

God made you so that your feelings didn't flip from one extreme to the other too quickly. Your body wasn't made for that.

Ever ride a roller coaster that you probably shouldn't have? Ever been in a near car accident? Sometimes, you're shaken for a long time. Ever worked out or done some manual labor and over-extended? You feel immediate relief when you stop working, but it can take days to recover. Often, you feel worse the second or third day after you over-extended.

Those of you that have carried things for a long time, give your emotions a little time. They'll come around. You don't have to strain or strive. You don't have to "whup" them into shape. Ever see an apple tree straining to pop out on apple? Of course not! The fruit of the Spirit is just that - FRUIT. Fruit grows because of what you planted, not because of self-control. In fact, self-control IS a fruit of the Spirit.

Your emotions are good barometer for what you were saying, believing, and experiencing….several days ago.

Principal: God will cause your thoughts to line up with His will.

Proverbs 16:3 says, *"Commit your works to the Lord and your plans will be established."*

But I prefer the Amplified Version:

"Roll your works upon the Lord [commit and trust them wholly to Him; He will cause your thoughts to become agreeable to His will, and] so shall your plans be established and succeed."

Principal: *You can't cast your emotions on the Lord, so don't try.*

So many times, we try to cast the feeling of anxiety on the Lord. You can't cast emotions on anyone. That's not what the Bible is instructing. Just cast the responsibilities over on the Lord that were HIS to begin with. Your emotions will follow shortly. And God will line your thoughts up with His will.

Day 15

"He leadeth me beside the still waters..."

IT IS NOT OUR JOB TO BE SPIRITUALLY CODEPENDENT

Several years ago, right after my computer lab experience with the Lord, I began a very different journey which will probably be another book someday. One of my teachers, Patrice, invited Tammy and me to her wedding. She was and is a dear friend and an outstanding educator. Life had thrown her a few curves, and she found herself single after many years of marriage. Appreciative of us being a support (I'm not sure I did all that much) through her divorce and then eventually meeting Joe, her soon to be new husband, she included us on the short list of invitees. The wedding was beautiful though small, and the service combined the wedding and reception into one event. Attendees were seated at round tables during the entire ceremony and celebration. Later, Patrice confessed that seating us next to her therapist at the reception "might" have been strategic.

Therapy had such a bad stigma among the Christian circles I grew up in. That stigma still exists today. It wasn't just that we thought therapists were old prunes with glasses on the end of their noses, who asked patients laying on a couch questions like, "Were you breast-fed as a child?" It went much deeper. "Therapy is something for people who are into some really, really bad stuff. It's for people who don't know how to get past their problems, but they should know. They probably weren't raised right….or spanked enough as a kid."

Yea, that's pretty much what I thought. Being from rural, God-fearing Pentecostal Oklahoma, I was taught two things:

If the husband takes his place as the rightful head of the household and the wife submits to him, and if they discipline their kids through spanking, all problems are solved. The kids will grow up healthy and successful. As a youngster, any time I'd become aware of problems people had, whether in marriage, emotional health, conflict, addiction, etc, the blanket wisdom spoken about the situation was "the wife is probably not submitting to her husband" or "they probably aren't spanking their kids enough."

As a side note to further illustrate the beliefs surrounding Christians attending therapy, when my sweet mother found out I was going, she was fully supportive and glad of the health it was bringing. Still, she confessed, "I feel like it means I failed you."

So you can imagine my surprise at the wedding when I was introduced to Kate, the petite redhead seated to my left who was also Patrice's therapist. She and her husband didn't look a day over thirty, and I suspected they both modeled for clothing catalogs on the side.

After the wedding, Tammy said to me, "I think I'd like to go see Kate." That was the beginning of a journey that saved both of us….and our marriage. It wasn't long before we were both seeing Kate regularly, as a couple and individually.

Shortly into our first few sessions, Kate identified that we were both very codependent. I was floored! I had to ask for a definition, because I always thought codependency was when people got together and did drugs. So you can imagine my surprise. "I don't do drugs, Kate!" I said flatly.

According to Merriam-Webster, *codependency* is *"a psychological condition or a relationship in which a person manifesting low self-esteem and a strong desire for approval has an unhealthy attachment to another person and places the needs of that person before his or her own."*

It was a little hard to swallow, but Kate expertly coached us into recognition and ultimately health. We were so burdened with the approval and happiness of others that we had placed the whole of our joy on it. It's amazing how one can live in the bondage of codependency and not even know it. How? We learn it. We are taught it.

A little side note: Spiritual abusers, insecure leaders, and even wolves in sheep's clothing who are in Christian leadership positions seek out spiritually codependent people to be on their "team" because they are easily controlled. People starved for approval will do most any task and take great abuse in exchange for approval. I know. I've been one starved for approval.

It was in the middle of one of these first sessions that Kate made an amazing statement. I don't know if she realized how impactful it was at the time. She said, "If you're not careful, you can even become codependent on God."

Codependent….on *GOD*? I thought we were supposed to depend on Him!

While we must recognize that it's God's job to lead as stated in Day 5, spiritual codependency actually works against His leading. God is not looking to control or manipulate us like an insecure leader would. He empowers us. A person who is constantly fearful he won't hear God correctly or that he'll make a wrong decision is actually keeping God from doing His job.

Many of us have served under leaders who are passive-aggressive or overbearing. We were expected to walk on eggshells or figure out the meaning behind all the passive-aggressive non-verbals.

God is neither passive-aggressive nor overbearing. He's not looking for relationship where people are running around like headless chickens, begging for affirmation and approval at every turn.

Father God is the the most loving and affirming person that exists or has ever existed. He IS love. And 1 John 4:18 tells us that His perfect love drives out fear. The one who fears is not perfected in love. You can't earn His approval. You already have it! He is FOR you. He's not "going be for you one day." He is FOR YOU RIGHT NOW! You are seated in heavenly places with Him. He loves to surround you with His lovingkindness.

Are you afraid you're not going to hear Him? Are you afraid you're going to make a mistake? Are you convinced you're not as good or holy as other people, and God surely won't come spend time with you? Do you believe Father God is mad at you are displeased with you? Do you fret over decisions because you fear making the wrong one?

These are all signs of spiritual codependency. And it is NOT what God wants from us.

Psalm 27:13-14 - "I would have despaired (codependency) unless I had believed I would see the goodness of the Lord in the land of the living. Wait for the Lord; Be strong, let your heart take courage; Yes, wait for the Lord."

"He restoreth my soul..."

"He restores my soul" in Psalm 23 means to 'bring back, restore, refresh, or repair."

Have you noticed anything yet about this roadmap for letting God spend time with you? First, you must realize He is your Shepherd. After that, God goes to work. He makes you lie down. Why? Because it puts you in right relationship with Him. It puts you in a position where He can take your burdens. The first thing He is interested in is you taking a position of rest; then He lifts all your burdens. Once He does that, He begins a process of renewal, refreshment, and repair.

IT'S GOD'S JOB TO WASH YOU

In John 13, Jesus did something that totally shocked the disciples. He took off His clothes, wrapped a towel around His waist, and began to wash His disciples' feet.

When it was Peter's turn, Peter protested. "Lord, are You going to wash my feet?"

"You won't understand now, Peter, but you will later," said Jesus.

Peter exclaimed, "Never shall you wash my feet!"

This is us. We do this to God all the time. It's because we think we're being so humble. But really, we are in full-fledged pride.

IT'S OUR JOB TO LET HIM

Jesus makes a statement that is mind-blowing. "If you don't let me wash your feet, Peter, YOU HAVE NO PART WITH ME." That's a fairly strong statement for Jesus to make. It wasn't that Jesus' feelings were hurt and so He was threatening to withdraw His friendship. Jesus was teaching Peter about how to have relationship with Him.

You see, Jesus wasn't washing His disciples' feet because He was being nice. He was washing their feet because He was personifying the Father. And it's the Father's job to wash your feet.

When is the last time you began your devotion by just simply laying down? When is the last time you let God wash your feet?

What do you think would happen if Jesus appeared in the room where you are right now? Do you think He would be displeased with you? Do you think He would wait for YOU to do something? Think about it for a minute.

I can tell you what Jesus would do. He would run to you. He would begin to encourage you to lie down. After you assumed your correct position, He would begin to wash your feet, lift your burdens, and refresh your soul.

IT'S GOD'S JOB TO SING OVER YOU

"You are my hiding place; You preserve me from trouble; You surround me with songs of deliverance."
- Psalm 32:7

"The Lord your God is with you, the Mighty Warrior who saves. He will take great delight in you; in His love He will no longer rebuke you,

but will rejoice over you with singing." - Zephaniah 3:17

Singing was never meant to be a one-way street. It's something God designed to be shared in an intimate relationship. He's the one who leads it. Did you think God created something like singing only to never participate? That's you thinking like a servant. You aren't a servant. You are a son of God and the bride of Christ. Yes, like Jesus, you take on the attitude of a servant in obedience to any command He gives. But that's not WHAT you are.

He rejoices and sings over you. All the time. It's so loud and consuming that it completely surrounds you. What do you think He is singing? He's saying things that bring deliverance. He's declaring His lovingkindness for you.

When is the last time you heard God sing over you? Are you letting Him?

Someone may ask, "Josh, how do I let God sing over me? If God is singing to me, it would seem hard to miss."

Really? Have you ever missed a turn in route to a destination? Have you ever failed to hear something your spouse or child said to you, even when they are within a few feet of you? Ever missed a meeting at work or a sale at the department store?

Distraction. Not listening. Not knowing it's there and available. It happens all the time. Realize God is singing to you and His songs are FOR you. You'll hear them. It's not hard. He created you for this very purpose!

SECRET #2

"He leadeth me in paths of righteousness..."

YOU BECOME LIKE YOUR FRIEND THROUGH INTIMACY

Day 17

This is one of the most misunderstood concepts in Christianity today. The truths revealed though Secret #2 will be very challenging for some readers, and I expect it will make some people plain angry. That's OK. Jesus made people angry all the time.

"And he said, "There was a man who had two sons. And the younger of them said to his father, 'Father, give me the share of property that is coming to me.' And he divided his property between them. Not many days later, the younger son gathered all he had and took a journey into a far country, and there he squandered his property in reckless living. And when he had spent everything, a severe famine arose in that country, and he began to be in need. So he went and hired himself out to one of the citizens of that country, who sent him into his fields to feed pigs. And he was longing to be fed with the pods that the pigs ate, and no one gave him anything.
"But when he came to himself, he said, 'How many of my father's hired servants have more than enough bread, but I perish here with hunger! I will arise and go to my father, and I will say to him, "Father, I have sinned against heaven and before you. I am no longer worthy to be called your son. Treat me as one of your hired servants."' And he arose and came to his father. But while he was still a long way off, his father saw him and felt compassion, and ran and embraced him and kissed him. And the son said to him, 'Father, I have sinned against heaven and before you. I am no longer worthy to be called your son.' But the father said to his servants, 'Bring quickly the best robe, and put it on him, and put a ring on his hand, and shoes on his feet. And bring the

fattened calf and kill it, and let us eat and celebrate. For this my son was dead, and is alive again; he was lost, and is found.' And they began to celebrate." - Luke 15:11-24 ESV

Remember this story? Of course we do. Most of us readily identify with the prodigal son. He was young and independent. He made bad choices and he burned a lot of bridges. It took a while for him to hit bottom. Even then, he didn't want to admit it.

Finally, he decided to face reality. Things weren't getting better. As he stared down at a pig trough, he realized there was a path to some relief. So, he forged a plan and started home.

Laudation! Applause! I can almost hear Chris Daughtry singing in the background. All sinners should do the same! Yes, this is the perfect attitude for all those caught in the cords of sin. It's the ultimate illustration for an alter call!

Right? Wrong.

Principle: You can't earn anything from the Lord, especially forgiveness.

Firstly, the son was on his way home...for FOOD!

"How many of my father's hired servants have more than enough bread, but I perish here with hunger!" - Luke 15:17.

He wasn't heading home to restore relationship. He wasn't going home to the place where he belonged, where love had always been enough for him. He wasn't going home to take his role.

Secondly, he was planning to earn the food!

"Treat me as one of your hired men." - Luke 15:19 ESV

How many of you have been there? How many are there right now? Sin in your life? Have you hit bottom? Let me guess: You've promised to do better. You'll read your Bible more. You'll pray more. You'll choose to forgive someone.

And, thus, begins the cycle that will once again end in failure and frustration. It's called pride. And God resists the proud. He doesn't resist the stinky, nasty, dirty sinner. He doesn't resist the one who is still struggling with drugs. He doesn't resist the one struggling with pornography. He doesn't resist the one struggling with anger and unforgiveness.

The prodigal son was in a really bad place. We picture that he was probably dirty and oh so sinful! But THE SIN WASN'T THE PROBLEM. (Mic check. Pow! Pow!) Sin wasn't the problem.

Principle: Trying to be worthy before you have fellowship with God is pride, and it will keep Him from being able to spend time with you.

Thirdly, the son resisted receiving the Father's love. He kept claiming he wasn't worthy. Thankfully, the Father completely ignored that.

Look at what the father did:

1. He ran to his son. He hugged and kissed him.

Principle: God isn't mad at you about your mistakes.

2. He ignored the foolish things the son was saying and commanded Him to be clothed: A robe on his shoulders, a ring on his finger, and shoes on his feet.

Principle: God is much more interested in assuring you of His love than He is correcting your attitudes and behavior.

3. He commanded the best calf be prepared and that celebration begin.

Principle: God is much more interested in provision and restoration than correcting your mistakes.

Do you think that the son was completely sinless? Do you think he was finished with all his addictions and hang-ups?

No. He wasn't.

"Yeah, Josh, but that son's heart was in the right place. He was so repentant. He was finally humbled and willing to be a servant."

Yeah, you've been to a lot of the same churches I attended, because that is the same God-awful nonsense I heard all my life. That's right, it's God-awful because it paints a picture of God as awful and of pride as a correct response.

You see, God can deal with sin. He can heal your body and transform your mind. He can break all your addictions. But He won't do it apart from you playing your role. He won't give you rest, healing, provision, and transformation unless you lie down.

"Why, Josh? Why is lying down and waiting the only thing God requires of us?"

BECAUSE HE PUT YOU HERE FOR RELATIONSHIP! And He's not going to give you any of those things apart from it.

Love. Assurance. Rest. Restoration. Provision. Fellowship. It was well after the son received these that transformation began to happen. It takes time to transform the junk in our lives. And the Father is completely fine with it.

God longs to celebrate, fellowship with, and sing over His children. My mom called it "making whoopee." The result of Him doing these things: we become like Him. He's not surprised about the sin in our life.

Come on. Let God make whoopee over you!

Day 18

I made a statement earlier that may have given you pause. I've listed it here as a principle.

Principle: God is much more interested in having relationship with you than He is correcting any wrong behavior or attitude.

I think a lot of you might be struggling with Day 17. Why? We're taught the opposite. The church has told us the opposite. We're taught that we have to get all the sin out of our heart before God will spend time with us. We're taught we need Him to "create in us a clean heart" before we can enjoy His presence. We must repent so that "times of refreshing will come from the presence of the Lord." But the truth is, you can't get the sin out of your life. You can't. Go ahead and try. If you could, the old covenant wouldn't have been done away with.

You don't believe that God is more interested in spending time with you than getting sin out of your life? Let me show you some scriptures and you can decide for yourself. I've already shown you the principle in the story of the prodigal son. Let's look at three more instances which illustrate or instruct us how to spend time with God.

1. Matthew 6: 9-13 *"Pray then like this: "Our Father in heaven, hallowed be your name. Your kingdom come, your will be done, on earth as it is in heaven. Give us this day our daily bread, and forgive us our debts, as we also have forgiven our debtors. And lead us not into temptation, but deliver us from evil."*

2. Psalm 23: 1-3 *"The Lord is my shepherd; I shall not want. He makes me lie down in green pastures. He leads me beside still waters. He restores my soul. He leads me in paths of righteousness for his name's sake."*

3. James 4:7-8 *"But he gives more grace. Therefore, it says, "God opposes the proud but gives grace to the humble." Submit yourselves therefore to God. Resist the devil, and he will flee from you. Draw near to God, and he will draw near to you. Cleanse your hands, you sinners, and purify your hearts, you double-minded."*

Let's break each one of these down. You might be amazed at how they line up.

1. He reveals His nature. He's not mad at you.

2. He seeks to get you in a place of relationship, which is you laying down and receiving.

3. He gives you the provision of His Presence and daily needs.

4. He begins transforming you into the image of Christ.

	Matthew 6	Psalm 23	James 4	Practical Revelation
1	Our Father	My Shepherd	God gives grace	God's Nature
2	Thy will be done	He makes me lie down	Submit to God	Get into your role
3	Give us our daily bread	He restores my soul	He will draw near to you	Benefits of relationship
4	Forgive us our debts	Guides in paths of righteousness	Cleanse your hands	God transforming you

Can you see it? Correcting your behavior, your attitudes, your deficiencies - that's way on down the priority list. This is the list of priorities and how they rank.

It's so important you see a biblical foundation for this principle. I don't want you to believe these principles because I say them. I want you to believe the Bible. If I'm telling you anything that doesn't line up with scripture, throw it away! I've shown four examples so far: Luke 15, Matthew 6, Psalm 23, and James 4.

Over the next few days, we'll look at even more passages to illustrate the truths of Secret #2.

Day 19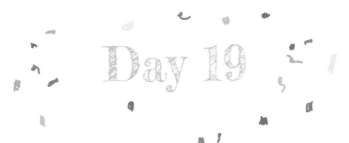

God is more interested in having relationship with you than He is correcting your behavior. Why?

Fellowship is what brings about the fruit of behavior correction!

This is true even of Christians! Where did we get the belief that Christians don't mess up? Christians can make big mistakes! Did your children make a mistake after they were born? Of course they did. In that illustration, we see mistakes as part of the learning process.

You'll notice that I tell a lot of stories about my parents. Subconsciously, I may be enjoying a little payback. As a PK (pastor's kid) there was no shortage of them using me in sermon illustrations, no matter how embarrassing the story may have been. Both my parents preached, so for me, it was a double whammy! But the truth is, my parents did some very story-worthy things. My dad made a word-slip in a sermon one time. And there was no running from it.

I'll never forget it. I was sitting on the front row of our little church in Holdenville, Oklahoma on Resurrection Sunday. I could literally feel the congregation gasp when dad informed them that Mary was the first person Jesus saw after His erection.

There was no hiding from it. There was no escaping it.

Of course, everyone knew what he meant to say. But still, he was embarrassed beyond words.

Have you ever done something from which you feel there's no escape? What Dad did was funny and totally forgivable. But we've all done worse things. Some things we're still hiding from, struggling with, or being totally beaten-up by.

The devil uses our past to beat us up. Then Christians come along and help him. Somehow, many Christians think only the sin we committed before becoming born again is totally forgiven and under the blood of Jesus. But IF CHRISTIANS SIN, whoa Nelly! It's an entirely different story! You have to do some real penance in that case!

And heaven forbid you get a divorce! That's certainly the unforgivable sin in the eyes of many denominations!

The Bible illustrates something completely different. While we are on the path to spiritual health, God doesn't expect we'll be sin-free after we're saved.

As I already stated, Christians can make BIG mistakes. But they don't have to ruin your life!

Principle: God doesn't expect you to never sin after you're born again.

But He does expect something: You to fit into your role. Why? All together now: *relationship!*

Principle: God desires to turn ANY mistake around for good.

But He will only do it if you fit into YOUR role.

Principle: It's not the size of the mistake that prevents God from healing and turning it for good. It's whether you continue relationship and fellowship.

Not convinced? We'll look at passage tomorrow to further illustrate.

Day 20

The whole chapter of 1 John 1 used to leave me in a state of panic.

"That which we have seen and heard we proclaim also to you, so that you too may have fellowship with us; and indeed our fellowship is with the Father and with his Son Jesus Christ. And we are writing these things so that our joy may be complete. This is the message we have heard from him and proclaim to you, that God is light, and in him is no darkness at all. If we say we have fellowship with him while we walk in darkness, we lie and do not practice the truth. But if we walk in the light, as he is in the light, we have fellowship with one another, and the blood of Jesus his Son cleanses us from all sin. If we say we have no sin, we deceive ourselves, and the truth is not in us. If we confess our sins, he is faithful and just to forgive us our sins and to cleanse us from all unrighteousness. If we say we have not sinned, we make him a liar, and his word is not in us." - 1 John 1:3-10

Well, I'm pretty much toast. How about you? If I walk in any darkness, I'm a liar. I know I have darkness in my life. I know I've made mistakes. I don't walk in God's pure light all the time. I'M TOAST!

That's how I used to read this passage. Maybe you have too. I was getting caught up because I thought 'light' represented holiness in this passage. I thought it represented sinlessness and darkness represented sin. Therefore, if I ever sin, I'm not walking in the light and I'm not cleansed of sin.

Let's walk through it correctly together.

Firstly, John makes plain the reason he was writing. It happens to be a theme of this book and the reason God put us here on earth: relationship and fellowship.

"That which we have seen and heard we proclaim also to you, so that you too may have fellowship with us; and indeed our fellowship is with the Father and with his Son Jesus Christ." - 1 John 1:3

John was showing us how to have relationship with God!

Secondly, light is not talking about sinlessness here. In fact, John plainly says if we claim not to have sin, we are lying!

Truth: 'Light' in 1 John 1 represents transparency, openness, and nothing hidden. It does not represent holiness.

You see, God is holy, but that's not characterized by light. Light characterizes the fact that God is open and not hiding. We'll talk more about that in Secret #3. John encourages us to walk in the light.

Does that sound like anything? Doesn't it sound like lying down? It's being vulnerable and open, and in a place to receive. John said if we walk in the light, in openness and transparency before God, something happens!

1. We have fellowship.

You see? God is much more intent on restoring fellowship than dealing with sin and mistakes. Because the fellowship is what brings the fruit of sinlessness.

2. Then the blood of Jesus cleanses us from all sin.

You see, if light were holiness, we wouldn't need the blood to cleanse us after were ALREADY WALKING IN IT! But

John said we walk in the light (lie down), have fellowship, and then the blood cleanses us. If we say we have no sin after we are already in the light, John says we're lying. But, after we're already in the light and enjoying fellowship, if we confess our sins, He is faithful and just to forgive AND CLEANSE US OF ALL UNRIGHTEOUSNESS!

And what was John showing us in all of this? He was showing us how to have fellowship with the Father and the Son.

Principle: God expects relationship after we are born again, not 'never sinning'. Fellowship grows the fruit of self-control.

Isn't that beautiful? And it's a process. We don't have to run and confess sin to get God's presence. He doesn't withhold His presence because of sin. We humble ourselves. We lie down. We get transparent in the light. He fellowships with us. He cleanses us. Then He starts talking to us about what needs to change. We confess and believe. We are transformed. If we sin, we run back to the fellowship.

Principle: The danger of sin is not that God can't forgive it. The danger is that you won't run back to the light of fellowship.

We don't have to be sinless to have fellowship. We have to walk in the light. Why? Because when we walk in the light, we have fellowship. And THEN the blood of Jesus comes and cleanses us from ALL sin.

Even the sins from AFTER we were saved.

Still don't believe God is more concerned about fellowship than dealing with sin? I challenge you to get before Him and ask.

Day 21

Principle: Sin does not keep God from running to spend time with his child.

One evening I was sitting at our kitchen bar. Our Natalie was in fifth grade at the time. "Daddy?" I could hear the emotion in her voice.
I turned to see my little girl with big tears welling from her eyes.

"What's wrong, babe?"

"I'm scared. I think I accidentally stuck my middle finger in the air…WAAAHHH!" She burst into tears.

My mind began to whirl as I encapsulated her in my arms. Where in the world did she even hear about the middle finger? She'd been in a private Christian school since pre-K. (And we know that no "sinful" things like knowledge of flipping the bird exist in a *Christian* school.)

"What's wrong with sticking up your middle finger? Who told you that was bad?" I asked.

"Sally said it was REALLY, REALLY bad if you stick out your middle finger," she sobbed.

"Well then, honey, daddy does really, really bad things every time he's stuck in traffic!" I'm kidding. I didn't say that. I don't flip people off. Well, not externally anyway.

I took a moment to process the information.

"Babe, I don't think you can accidentally stick your middle finger up. It's called flipping someone off, and it has to do with intent or it doesn't count." She wasn't buying it. I took a different approach. As an educator, I welcomed the teaching moment. "Ok, honey, so what if you did? What if you stuck your middle finger up?"

"Oh, it's really bad!" She began sobbing again.
"Honey, the Bible is very clear that when we sin, we have an 'Advocate with the Father.' The blood of Jesus cleanses us from all sin." She calmed a little, and I prayed with her.
 After some further assurance from me, she seemed to let it go. I assumed she was probably anxious about something else. Maybe just tired.

It couldn't have been more than a couple of days later. She came to me again in tears with the weight of condemnation on her shoulders. "I was brushing my hair in the mirror," she sniffed, "and I'm pretty sure my middle finger went up while the other fingers stayed down."

I paused, a little surprised this was again bringing her such guilt. "Babe, that's not flipping someone off." She wasn't convinced. Her friend said the middle finger was bad and, in her mind, it might has well have come from the writings of the Holy King James Bible! (Because that's the only true, infallible translation, right?)

I realized I would have to take a dramatic approach. "What do you think is going to happen if you lift your middle finger? Is lightning from heaven going to strike you?" She didn't quite know how to answer, but she replied that it would just be really bad. "Follow me," I said. I led her to the back porch. The night sky was full of bright stars. There was nothing to hide the eyes of God from seeing the great sin we were about to commit. I extended both my middle fingers and waved them toward the heavens with arms fully stretched. I instructed her to do the same. With a brief hesitation, she obeyed.

"Now," I said, "did lightning strike us?" She shook her head and started to smile a little. "Really? No wrath from heaven?" She shook her head. "So you see, babe, everything is OK. You didn't 'flip someone off.' And even if you did, there is forgiveness." I prayed with her. Once again, the weight of guilt she was feeling subsided. I chuckled to myself a little. I was also humored and proud of my fatherly teaching moment. I never dreamed I'd be having my daughter wave her middle fingers in the air.

My pride at being able to father my daughter through emotional crises quickly faded. Only a few days later, we were replaying the same scenario. My lessons and illustrations weren't helping this time. Not at all. I was dumbfounded.

When I attended a previously scheduled therapy session the next day, my Natalie's dilemma was still weighing on my mind. As we were wrapping up the session, I asked my therapist about it. After listening to a brief synopsis of the story, she said, "The next time this happens, ask Natalie what she is feeling. Once she tells you, ask her to think of another time or, if possible, the first time she can remember having that same feeling. Give her time. She may not have the answer immediately."

That very night, it happened again. Natalie came to me extremely upset. She thought she might have accidentally raised her middle finger at school while standing in the lunch line.

"Come sit down, babe," I instructed. She obeyed. "Tell me what you are feeling right now." She thought for a moment.

"I feel very guilty!" she explained.

"Ok, I want you to do something. Think of the first time you can ever remember feeling that same kind of guilty you are feeling now. Even if it's a time when I did something. If I spanked you and shouldn't have, or got mad at you, I want you to be honest and tell me. Anything you say is OK." She nodded and said she would need to think about it. It calmed her that there was something to do as part of diagnosing the problem. She left the room.

Five minutes later, she came back. "I thought of something but I'm not sure if it's anything important." This relieved me a little. I was sure she was going to remember a time when I was too tough on her. "My teacher was teaching a lesson, and told us that when we sin, a wall comes between us and God."

Time stood still for a moment. I will never forget it. It was all I could do to contain the holy anger boiling inside me.

WHAT IN THE WORLD? She had not learned that from us.

Quick side bar. Natalie has had wonderful teachers, all who love God and love her immensely. I cast no judgement on any of them. It's not certain what the teacher actually said. I'm not certain of the context. We didn't feel it necessary to investigate. The important thing was what Natalie heard, even if she heard it incorrectly.

"Run that by me again," I instructed Natalie as calmly as I could.

"When we sin, a wall (She used her hands to illustrate the wall of judgment that forms between God and the one who sins.) forms between us and God." There was so much wrong in that statement, I didn't even know where to begin.

"And you *believe* that? You *believe* that a wall forms between you and God when you stick up your middle finger?"

"Oh yes! No evil or sin or unholiness can exist in God's Presence." I stepped up to the plate and tightened my grip on the bat. I was gonna knock this one out of the park!

"Well," I shrugged, "too bad Satan doesn't know that."

"What?" She raised one eyebrow.

"Yea, too bad Satan doesn't know that. He's in God's Presence all the time."

"Really!?!"

"Yep. In the book of Job and also in the book of Zechariah, Satan stands in God's Presence all the time. You see, the fact that no evil can stand in God's Presence sounds spiritual, but it's not in the Bible…at least not in that context. Think of Jesus. He ate with sinners all the time. Wasn't Jesus God?"

"Uh..yes." She said, starting to smile. I could see the lie being broken and the fear leaving.

"Jesus lives in you by the Holy Spirit. How can a wall separate you from Him? You are more of a daughter to God than you are to me, although that may be hard to picture. I would never kick you out of my house for doing something wrong. And nothing you could do would make you stop being my daughter. Nothing you could do could stop me pursuing you. Am I a better father than Father God? No! He's the best Father of all, and He's is WAY more gracious than I am!"

The joy was beaming from her face at this point. The grip of fear and guilt broke off her in that moment and never even remotely plagued her again.

It's amazing how one phrase heard at one moment can cause great problems. It can hold you in a form of bondage. But that's not the only lesson from this story. Like Natalie, we've been taught that we are separated from God any time we mess up, and we have to do some kind of works or performance to earn back His Presence and favor.

Nothing could be further from the truth.

Day 22

I've probably heard a hundred sermons about the parable of the sower in Mark 4. This parable is also contained in Matthew 13 and Luke 8. If you are unfamiliar with this story, briefly reading those three accounts of the parable will be helpful before reading today's devotion. I've inserted a small excerpt here:

And He said to them, "Do you not understand this parable? How then will you understand all the parables? The sower sows the word. And these are the ones along the path, where the word is sown: when they hear, Satan immediately comes and takes away the word that is sown in them. And these are the ones sown on rocky ground: the ones who, when they hear the word, immediately receive it with joy. And they have no root in themselves, but endure for a while; then, when tribulation or persecution arises on account of the word, immediately they fall away. And others are the ones sown among thorns. They are those who hear the word, but the cares of the world and the deceitfulness of riches and the desires for other things enter in and choke the word, and it proves unfruitful. But those that were sown on the good soil are the ones who hear the word and accept it and bear fruit, thirtyfold and sixtyfold and a hundredfold."
- Mark 4:13-20 ESV

It's pretty clear that the seed represents the Word of God and the different settings or soils represent man's response to the Word. In Matthew 13, Jesus indicates that the Word which was stolen by the evil one was first "sown in his (man's) heart." So it could be said that the different soils represent man's heart.

IT'S NOT YOUR JOB TO "GET YOUR HEART RIGHT" OR GET THE SIN OUT OF YOUR LIFE

"You gotta get your heart right!" I'd hear this from the Sunday morning pulpit all the time. Or "You gotta get the stones out of your heart!" Supposedly the stones represent unforgiveness, pride, etc. And there might well be some application of those ideas.

Still, Jesus never said anything like that in reference to this parable. He never said to get the stones out. He never said to get the thorns out.

Here is the one thing He said to do:

"Pay attention to what you hear: with the measure you use, it will be measured to you, and still more will be added to you. For to the one who has, more will be given, and from the one who has not, even what he has will be taken away."
- Mark 4:24-25 ESV

So what is the command here? What is it that Jesus said we are to do? LISTEN! He didn't say to get your heart right or get the stones out. He said to LISTEN. And guess what? As much as you listen (the measure you use), that's how much you'll receive.

Let me give you an example. You decide to bake a cake, and it calls for 1/2 cup of flour. You go to the kitchen drawer and pull out 1/2 measuring cup. After dipping it in the bag of flour, you bring out as much as you can. How much flour do you have? Half a cup, right? WRONG! YOU HAVE MORE THAN THAT!

My mom taught me this. You have to rake the flour to even with the top of the measuring cup. Any flour that's piled above the rim of the measuring cup is extra. I got a lot of recipes wrong because of misunderstanding this.

Do you see it now? Jesus said, "*With the measure you use, it will be measured to you, and still more will be added to you.*" Like dipping the cup in flour, you'll get what you measured for and even more!!!

Principle: As much as you listen to the Lord and to the Word, that's how much you'll receive, plus a little more.

So, what are we supposed to do? LISTEN! Doesn't it fit better with what I illustrated in earlier devotions is our job? Wait. Seek. Hope. Meditate. Mutter the Word.

I've heard well-intentioned, sincere pastors and preachers telling people to get their heart right and to get the sin out. I've watched people trying so hard to get the sin out and become continually frustrated. Why? They're doing God's job.

The Word will do the work. Ever notice that LOVE is a fruit of the spirit? Ever notice that lovingkindness is a fruit? Goodness is a fruit. Here's the big one....wait for it....SELF CONTROL IS A FRUIT OF THE SPIRIT!

Principle: You can't will yourself to have fruit. THE WORD WILL DO THE WORK!

"But Josh, can't I will myself to stop sinning?" Yes. It'll work for a little while. You can will yourself to exercise and diet. You can will yourself not to watch that movie. You can try to will yourself to forgive. But it will be short-lived. Go ahead and try. If it works for you, hat's off to ya! I applaud you. Really, I do!

But the fact is, if you could will yourself to not sin, there wouldn't have been need for a new and better covenant. We could still live in the old.

I like what Kenneth Copeland says: "Don't try to quit that habit. Get your mind renewed in the Word, and that habit will quit you!"

So what is my will power for? Don't I use it?

OF COURSE! You will yourself to do YOUR JOB. Will yourself to meditate on what the Word says about who the Shepherd is. Will yourself to wait. Will yourself to hope and seek. The fruit will come.

And you know what? Like Jesus said, you'll find this is a yoke that is easy and light. The yoke of trying to stop sinning is heavy and frustrating. Why? BECAUSE IT'S NOT YOUR JOB!

Secret #3

INTIMATE FRIENDS DON'T HIDE ANYTHING FROM EACH OTHER

Day 23

God made us to desire intimate relationship. The most intimate relationship on earth happens in marriage between husband and wife. As I've already alluded to and will continue to explain, the marriage relationship is only a type and shadow of the real thing: the relationship we have with God.

Why is marriage the most intimate relationship between humans on earth? It's a relationship of complete openness. Husband and wife get fully naked before each other. And they become physically and spiritually one.

Relationships are built on trust. Trust allows for complete openness. This happens in a healthy marriage.

God wired us to desire intimacy. He wired us to want to see nakedness in an intimate relationship. Men generally desire most to see women physically naked. Women generally long to see men emotionally naked.

Why? When your naked before someone, you are baring your most tender, sensitive parts. And you are communicating "I'm not holding anything back from you." It's stimulating, fulfilling, and fun!

And God fully intended it to be that way.

ITS GOD'S JOB TO GET NAKED

I realize this is a very bold statement. But it's true. He's not hiding anything. And He wants to reveal Himself to you in a way that draws you into intimacy with Him. But the thing is, He starts first. He gets real and open with you.

Why?

Principle: Vulnerability breeds trust.

Every great leader knows this and practices it, if they want to have followers. God is the best leader of all.

"Greater love has no one than this, that someone lay down his life for his friends. You are my friends if you do what I command you. No longer do I call you servants, for the servant does not know what his master is doing; but I have called you friends, for all that I have heard from my Father I have made known to you." - John 15:13-15

Jesus defined intimate friendship. It's laying down your life. It's giving yourself fully. And it holds nothing back. He said, "I've told you everything."

Principle: God isn't holding back.

One of the most misquoted passages is found in Isaiah 55. Things happen in life that people don't understand. Christians, particularly Christian leaders, often feel an obligation to have an answer for the seeming inexplicable curves that life throws.

"Well," they say, "His ways are higher than our ways and His thoughts are higher than our thoughts. As high as the heavens are above the earth, that's how much higher His ways are than ours. Who can fully know His ways?"

In other words, they imply that sometimes God just does things and doesn't explain why. And it's because it's so 'high', it's out of our reach to understand. It implies God's nature is to hold back.

I've heard this over and over. Maybe you have too.

The problem is, Isaiah 55 is saying the opposite! Isaiah was saying come and eat! Buy anything you want without money! Listen and seek the Lord, for His ways are higher! Let the wicked and unrighteous forsake their thoughts and ways, and come up to His because His thoughts are higher!

I encourage you to read this chapter! It's amazing how it has been twisted into an opposite meaning.

Isaiah 55 is not telling of God's untouchable, unreachable ways! IT IS AN INVITATION TO EXPERIENCE HIM FULLY!

Principle: You can't get more intimate than to be inside someone.

God gets naked with us. He doesn't hold back, as I'll explain in further days. But He didn't just redeem us and cause us to be born again. His purpose was to be inside us! Jesus prayed:

"I in them and You in Me, that they may be perfected in unity, so that the world may know that You sent Me, and loved them, even as You have loved Me." - John 17:23

God on the inside of us in perfect unity. And did you catch why God wanted to be on the inside? So that we may know He sent Jesus, and LOVED US AS MUCH AS HE LOVES JESUS!

God loves you as much as He loves Jesus!

WOW!

Day 24

"*And when he was alone, those around him with the twelve asked him about the parables. And he said to them, "To you has been given the secret of the kingdom of God, but for those outside everything is in parables, so that "'they may indeed see but not perceive, and may indeed hear but not understand, lest they should turn and be forgiven.'" - Mark 4:10-12 ESV*

Peter shrugged his shoulders as he padded the of outside his pockets. John turned his completely inside out. James dug through his satchel while several of Jesus' followers looked expectantly to the disciples for hidden treasure to be revealed at any moment. Several other disciples ribbed each other, turning their palms up as if to say, "Where the heck are you hiding it?"

Thomas whispered to John, "Did I miss something? He's always taking you, James, and Peter on 'special missions' up mountains and what not. Y'all been holdin' out on us? Where'd you hide the kingdom secret?"

Jesus indicated that the disciples, as well as his other followers, had been given the secret of the kingdom. The word translated 'secret' or 'mysteries' is the Greek word *mysterion*. Most of the time, it's translated into the singular case, not the plural. Jesus most likely wasn't talking about mysteries. He was probably talking about one secret, one mystery. Interesting. If the disciples had it, they didn't know it or couldn't find it. Because up to this point, they didn't have any more understanding about the parables than the multitudes!

This passage would always leave me tied up in knots. It didn't seem to match the nature of a good God. The way I read it, Jesus was talking cryptically to the multitudes, trying to veil the truth to fulfill the the scripture from Isaiah that certain people were destined not to believe. I basically thought Jesus was saying, "I'm talking in code so that people won't perceive, because if they did, I would have to forgive them." Then He was taking His select group aside and sharing secrets with them.

As a youngster, I was too scared to ask anybody, afraid that it might really be true: God wasn't good and He held back sometimes. Sermons I heard on the subject only seemed to confirm my fears. Was this really the nature of God revealed through Jesus?

Sitting in that middle school computer lab listening to the Lord, this was one of the passages He led me to. Here's how He opened my eyes to what was really going on in this story.

Principle: God isn't holding back revelation.

*"With many such parables he spoke the word to them, **as they were able to hear it**." - Mark 4:33 ESV*

Did you catch that? Jesus wasn't speaking as they WEREN'T able to hear it. He was speaking as much as they WERE able to hear. He wanted everyone to know the meaning of the parables. That's the purpose of parables: to make learning easy. He wasn't being cryptic.

Principle: The secret of the kingdom of God is relationship.

When asked about the parable, Jesus said that those asking had been given something. Already. Not going to give. It "has been given." The secret Jesus was referring to couldn't have been the meaning of the parable, because they didn't know the meaning. THE SECRET WAS THE RELATIONSHIP.

As I said earlier, the word *mysterion* is the Greek word translated "secret" or "mystery" in Mark 4, Luke 8, and Matthew 13 where the above story is recorded. The word appears several other times in the New Testament, but it is most often used by Paul in Ephesians.

*"And to make all men see what is the **fellowship** of the **mysterion**…" - Ephesians 3:9 KJV*

Can you have fellowship of a revelation? Can you have fellowship of a hidden meaning? No. Can you have fellowship of a relationship? YES! So, the secret or mystery is relationship.

In Ephesians 5, Paul goes into detail about marriage, explaining the role of the husband and the wife. Yet at the end of the explanation, he makes a fascinating statement:

*"This is a great **mysterion**: but I speak concerning Christ and the church." - Ephesians 5:32 KJV*

Marriage is a picture of Christ and the church! It is a sacred and intimate relationship. And it is a MYSTERY!

Principle: God reveals truth through intimacy.

Just like any relationship, guards are let down and truth is revealed through time and trust. In Mark 4, did you notice that Jesus didn't make any effort to explain the parables until the disciples asked about them? But it wasn't just the disciples! It was also those who were following Jesus. He was so thrilled they asked that He immediately told them they had the secret. Why? Because He wanted them to know what the secret was: relationship. Listen to how He teaches them:

"And he said to them, "Do you not understand this parable?
- Mark 4:13a ESV

I always thought Jesus was mildly rebuking them by this statement. Not so! He was explaining. It was a teaching moment.

"How then will you understand all the parables?"
- Mark 4:13b

In other words, Jesus was saying, "You don't understand on your own, do you? So what are you going to do in the future when you don't understand?"

The answer: "Ask." He was preparing them to have a relationship with the Holy Spirit. And what is the Holy Spirit's job?

According to John 16:13 ESV, Jesus said, "*I still have many things to say to you, but you cannot bear them now. When the Spirit of truth comes, he will guide you into all the truth...*"

Jesus had a LOT more to say. But the disciples couldn't bear it. Sound like the above story? But the Holy Spirit was sent to guide them into all truth, and remind them of what Jesus said.

You see? He wasn't wanting them to always know the answer. He was wanting them to know the secret. The secret is that through relationship, the revelation comes.

God isn't holding back. But He is a stickler about one thing: RELATIONSHIP!

Day 25

"Out of the ground Adonai, God, caused to grow every tree pleasing in appearance and good for food, including the tree of life in the middle of the garden and the tree of the knowledge of good and evil." – Genesis 2:9 (CJB)

If we're unsure of God's goodness, we won't trust Him as Shepherd. It will hinder our ability to let Him spend time with us. If we think He is holding back, we won't get transparent with Him.

I believe the enemy has gone way back to the very beginning, attempting to paint God as one Who is not good.

As a kid in Sunday School, I was taught about the garden of Eden. It's where God put Adam and Eve right after the Creation. They got to run around naked and not work, eating fruit that grew lusciously from trees. Well, that's the picture I got as a youngster anyway.

But God commanded them not to eat of the tree of the knowledge of good and evil. He told them they would die if they did.

Then the serpent came. He tempted Eve and she ate the 'forbidden' fruit and gave some to Adam who ate as well. Their eyes were suddenly opened and they realized they were naked. The Bible says they sewed fig leaves together to cover themselves.

Is that how you were taught?

You see, I was always taught that God put the tree of the knowledge of good and evil in the garden to test man. He supposedly had to make some way to give man 'free will'.

But this thinking presents several problems, and the Lord began to show me that the Bible illustrates something completely different.

1. **All the trees were good for food.**

ALL the trees, according to Genesis 2:9, were pleasing and good for food. Yes, the tree of the knowledge of good and evil was good for food.

2. **The Bible never calls the fruit forbidden.**

The truth is, God didn't tell them they couldn't eat of the tree. He said they couldn't EAT FREELY.

"The Lord God commanded the man, saying, "From any tree of the garden you may eat freely; but from the tree of the knowledge of good and evil you shall not eat, for in the day that you eat from it you will surely die."
- Genesis 2:16-17 NASB

God gave Adam and Eve permission to eat freely. This meant they could pick and eat from any tree except the tree of the knowledge of good and evil. But notice He didn't say the fruit was bad. He said they couldn't eat directly from the tree.

3. **The tree of the knowledge of good and evil and the tree of life were in the VERY CENTER of the garden.**

If something is at the center, it's pretty safe to assume it is the center of purpose.

Principle: God doesn't dress up evil as good to tempt you.

I don't believe God put the tree of the knowledge of good and evil in the garden as 'fake' food. I believe He wanted Adam and Eve to eat of it.

For what purpose did God create man? Intimacy. Relationship.

The tree of the knowledge of good and evil wasn't at the center of the garden to give man a choice. What a cruel thing to do! Dress up something supposedly evil as something so tempting and place it in the center as a constant temptation!

"Let no one say when he is tempted, "I am being tempted by God"; for God cannot be tempted by evil, and He Himself does not tempt anyone." – James 1:13

God wanted Adam and Eve to eat of the tree of the knowledge of good and evil. Do you think He never wanted them to know the difference between good and evil?

Of course He did. But this tree didn't represent law. And it didn't represent free will.

Truth: The tree of the knowledge of good and evil represented relationship.

Adam and Eve broke relationship. They didn't eat something poisonous and toxic. They ate something they weren't supposed to eat apart from relationship.

THAT'S WHY HE PUT IT AT THE CENTER!

If it was a reminder of anything, it was a reminder of relationship.

What did Adam and Eve cover? Their whole bodies? No. They covered their genitals. They covered their most intimate, sensitive parts.

Why? Not because they broke a law. They broke relationship. And it affected the intimacy between them.

You see, when God came walking in the garden in the cool of the evening, they hid in the trees. But right after they'd eaten, they hid their private parts from each other. God wasn't on the scene yet, so to speak.

I know a lot of people who think we'd all still be running around naked in the garden if Adam and Eve hadn't eaten of the fruit of this tree.

Do you really think God never wanted us to wear clothes? Do you know that Jesus wears clothes?

"And in the middle of the lampstands I saw one like a son of man, clothed in a robe reaching to the feet, and girded across His chest with a golden sash." – Revelation 1:13

Adam and Eve were created full grown. Ever think about that? But in their development of knowledge and understanding, they were probably very young. It was no different than a young toddler running around in his birthday suit. No one thinks it strange. Why? The toddler is young and innocent. But there comes a time when clothes are appropriate. Not because of shame. **But because parts of us are made to be revealed only within covenant!**

You see, God has things He reveals only in covenant relationship. God's plan was to sit down and feed them from the tree as they were ready to hear it.

This principle still applies today. It happens in the home. Parents take of the tree of the knowledge of good and evil and feed it to their children as they are ready. It should be in the center of the home. You don't need to teach a toddler about sex, even though sex is good. They aren't ready. They certainly aren't ready to hear about the evil in the world. You feed them as they are developmentally ready to eat it.

Many times, parents take the tree of the knowledge of good and evil and put it outside the home. They don't put it at the center. They don't put it as a marker of something to be eaten within covenant relationship! Unfortunately, Christians can even be guilty of this because of shame and wrong theology.

Parents, please talk to your kids about sex. Talk to them about intimacy. Isn't sex good? Do you want your kids to participate in it some day? Of course you do! But there is a healthy way to learn about sex. There is a healthy way to participate in one of the most beautiful things on earth.

If you take the tree and put it outside your home, never feeding it to your kids, they'll learn about it somewhere else. And you know what happens? Breakdown of relationship. Covering up. A seared conscience.

Satan convinced Eve that God was hiding something from her. He convinced Eve that God was holding back. And it led to Eve eventually covering up, and it hurt intimacy on every level.

He is still spreading that lie today. Satan is trying to convince people that God holds back.

But God is not holding back.

"He who did not spare His own Son, but delivered Him over for us all, how will He not also with Him freely give us all things?" -Romans 8:32

Principle: *If you think God is holding back from you, you'll put on fig leaves.*

God never changes. He's the same yesterday, today, and forever (Hebrews 13:8). He's always been good. Even back in the garden, it was always about relationship and sharing His best.

Ready to take off the fig leaves?

"Now his older son was in the field, and when he came and approached the house, he heard music and dancing. And he summoned one of the servants and began inquiring what these things could be. And he said to him, 'Your brother has come, and your father has killed the fattened calf because he has received him back safe and sound.' But he became angry and was not willing to go in; and his father came out and began pleading with him. But he answered and said to his father, 'Look! For so many years I have been serving you and I have never neglected a command of yours; and yet you have never given me a young goat, so that I might celebrate with my friends; but when this son of yours came, who has devoured your wealth with prostitutes, you killed the fattened calf for him.' And he said to him, 'Son, you have always been with me, and all that is mine is yours. But we had to celebrate and rejoice, for this brother of yours was dead and has begun to live, and was lost and has been found.'" - Luke 15:25-32

IT'S OUR JOB TO GET NAKED WITH GOD

There's probably no one I identify with more in the Bible than the prodigal son's brother. He represents people raised in church. Those of us who were raised in church have a tendency to try to earn God's favor and blessing.

This older brother did everything right. By his own admission, he served faithfully for years. He NEVER neglected his father's command.

How many of you identify? How many of you got burned by

church? You did everything you were 'supposed to do'. You tithed. You served. You were there every time the door was open. You went to all the camps and conferences. And after years, you feel empty-handed and empty-souled.

That was me back in the computer lab. I felt I had wasted so much time. I had done so much work and commitment only to have the same struggles and emptiness as everyone else.

But it gets worse for the older son. A sorry old failure like his little brother comes waltzing home looking like a hobo, and he gets all the attention, love, and blessing the older son was dreaming of.

I've thought it so many times prior to my computer lab experience: I should have spent time partying. I should've lived it up more. Here I am with nothing, and people who didn't get saved until recently have more blessing than me! What in the world, God?

Ever thought that?

The father in the story, being such a good father, finally comes out to the older brother who is too hurt and bitter to come in.

"All this time, Dad! All this time I've worked my butt off! And for what? You neglect me! You've held back from me!"

This part is very important. The older brother reveals two key points:

1. He admits, "You have never given me a young goat.." All these years and the older son had NEVER experienced fellowship!

2. He continued, "...so I might celebrate with my

friends." What was it the older brother wanted?
INTIMATE FRIENDSHIP!

Then the father makes a great statement:

"Son, all that I have is yours. It's been yours ALL ALONG!"

So why didn't the older son experience intimate friendship and fellowship? Because he was trying to earn it. He could've had intimate fellowship at any time, whenever he wanted.

Attempting to earn intimacy will actually hinder you from receiving it. Why? The father won't come do your job for you. He's waiting on you to fill your role.

Principle: You cannot earn intimate friendship or fellowship.

Wonder why people who've lived a rough, prodigal-type life come in to the kingdom of God and seem to have it better than those of us who have been 'saved' literally all of our lives? Because they know they can't earn it. It's easier for them to get in a position to receive.

God is not looking for people to serve more. Those of you who are reading this and have been burned or burnt-out in ministry, you were probably fed a lie. God does not grant fellowship to those who serve hard and work faithfully.

Principle: God grants intimate fellowship to those who get naked.

So, when is the last time you took the fig leaves off? When is the last time you came in from the 'field of serving' and accepted what has been yours all along?
"I don't know how to do that, Josh," you say.

I know you don't. We're not taught *how* to. And we're often taught it's not OK to get naked.

I'll explain more in the coming chapters, but here's what you do:

Get alone. Vomit it all out to God. Let loose with everything you're feeling. Don't hold back. Don't say what you think you are supposed to say. Get naked.

Then wait. He'll soon run with robe and ring in hand!

Day 27

My mom never used crass or vulgar language. My brothers and I were not even allowed to say words like 'butt". 'Bottom' was the proper reference for your hindquarters. I never heard my mom utter a curse word. In fact, I never even heard her slip with a replacement curse word, like 'dang it' or 'shoot'.

Except for one time.

My brother, Jason, and I had played outside in our good clothes, and we'd gotten them muddy. When I was elementary age, I had one set of 'good' clothes. At the beginning of the school year, we received a new pair of shoes and a new pair of jeans. That was supposed to last us for the year. Ruining those 'good' clothes was grounds for severe disciplinary action.

Having gone outside to enjoy some good ol' fashioned fun on our 40-acre farm without changing clothes, Jason and I soon realized we'd crossed a line after we both stumbled into a mud puddle. We decided it would be best to turn ourselves in and try to plead our case, so we slid in the back door of our mobile home, armed with excuses. Mom took one look at us lit in.

She was only a few words into her lecture when we both decided to interject, which in those days was known has 'talking back'. Mom quickly stifled the the talking back, elevating her voice to say, "SHUSH IT!"

The only problem was, in her frustration, she ran the words

together. By all appearances, mom had just gotten angry and yelled out the "s" word!

We all hesitated, staring at each other. Jason and I were jarred by the possibility and mom was obviously shaken. Somewhere in the distance a dog barked.

Jason and I finally burst out in howling laughter as we scurried through the back door, sure that mom would be right behind us with the belt. But she didn't follow us. I guess she was too ashamed.

Mom was the queen of word-bungles. Her modest and polite manner is what made them seem so funny. A few years ago, I was talking to her on the phone. We were discussing the fact that marriage brings opportunity for conflict. She stated flatly, "Yea, son, your father and I have been married 50 years and we still butt holes all the time." I'm pretty sure she meant to say butt heads, but much like the time mom said the "s" word, I busted out laughing.

Relationships bring conflict. As participants in a relationship, sometimes we butt heads, or we might even butt holes. Occasionally, we all can act like 'buttholes.'

Principle: Growth happens in and through relationships.

God created relationships. It is the reason He put us here. And He purposed that growth would happen through our relationship with Him. And it's the reason He didn't want Adam and Eve to partake of the tree of the knowledge of good and evil apart from Him.

"Abide in me, and I in you. As the branch cannot bear fruit by itself, unless it abides in the vine, neither can you, unless you abide in me. I am the vine; you are the branches. Whoever abides in me and I in him, he it is that bears much

fruit, for apart from me you can do nothing. "- John 15:4-5

But we don't only grow through our relationship with God. Growth happens through our relationships with each other. It's one of the reasons that the church is referenced collectively as 'the body.'

"From whom the whole body, joined and held together by every joint with which it is equipped, when each part is working properly, makes the body grow so that it builds itself up in love." - Ephesians 4:16

Fruit cannot be earned. You cannot work to get fruit. It happens as a result of intimacy. Pruning, however, is sometimes painful. It happens through conflict.

Principle: Growth doesn't happen apart from conflict.

Again, this is not to be confused with working or earning. It's pruning.

A good way to measure the healthiness of a relationship is to ask yourself, "When is the last time I've been challenged or had conflict?" Conflict is a key ingredient of a healthy relationship. Married couples who boast years of happy marriage without a cross word are either lying, or their marriage isn't growing.

I was taught the opposite. I was taught that if there was conflict, somebody must be in the wrong. But nothing could be further from the truth.

Scriptures can be over-emphasized in this area. But while Paul warned us against letting the sun go down on anger, and Jesus instructed us to forgive, He never purposed that we would have a life free from conflict.

Change is conflicting, and you can't go through any process of pruning without change. Pruning is a healthy and on-going process in the life of a Christian.

Principle: A relationship with God is a safe place to be raw.

Tell God how you are feeling in the midst of pruning. Conflict is healthy. It's healthy in your time with the Lord. It actually facilitates the pruning for you to talk honestly with Him about it.

It's God's job to lead us. It's His job to bear our burdens. It's totally HIS job to get the sin out of our life. But it's also His job to prune us.

It's our job to let Him. It's our job to wait on Him. It's our job to lay down.

Still, pruning can cause pain. So process it with Him! It's ok to let it all hang out. It's your job to be honest with Him!

Principle: God wants to process through pruning with you.

In the midst of all the up's and down's of life, His purpose is for you to walk though it with Him. So He has created relationship with Him to be a safe refuge.

As you'll see in the next chapter, it's ok to let words fly, purposefully or not (like my mom). In fact, it's very healthy. It's ok to butt heads or but holes.

It's what He wants you to do!

Day 28

Tent of Meeting. Pillar of cloud outside the door. Millions of people watching from a distance, then falling on their faces at the sight. God Himself talking to you face to face. God treating you like an intimate friend.

Joy unspeakable, right? Shouldn't you be swinging from the chandeliers?

Moses wasn't.

In Exodus 33, Moses had questions. He had concerns and frustrations. In Numbers 11, he was so depressed that he requested God to kill him. He wasn't being overly dramatic. He was at a place where death seemed like a comfort.

Healthy, intimate relationships are NOT characterized by never having a raw emotion. They aren't without nasty words.

Principle: You can't get naked without being honest.

That's what nakedness is. It's revealing who you are. It's showing, "This is what I really look like underneath. This is what's hidden in all the nooks and crannies."

God didn't talk intimately with Moses because he was chosen and foreordained. Moses didn't enjoy God's unveiled friendship because he was he was the leader of Israel.

Both enjoyed an intimate friendship because both of them got naked. And this means both were honest.

God isn't surprised by your nakedness. He's not offended if you let cuss words fly. That's right. It's not dirtying up His holiness.

Why? Because He knows what's there anyway. But when you bring it to Him, you are getting naked in the light. Isn't that what intimacy is? You are telling Him, "I'm not hiding."

And that's your job.

David was a man after God's own heart. Talk about someone with failures! He used his title to seduce a woman. He committed adultery. He ordered what resulted in mass murder to cover up the adultery. He tested God by counting his troops.

Pretty bad sins. Even after he knew the Lord!

But, hey, he didn't get a divorce! He could still be a licensed preacher with the Assemblies of God denomination.

David was known as a man after God's own heart. Not because he was chosen. Not because he was king. It was because he knew how to get naked. And HE LITERALLY DID when Israel brought the ark of the covenant back from into the house of God. He took off his robes and danced with all His might.

Read the Psalms. David was raw and honest with God.

Principle: *Your tent of meeting needs to be where others can't hear.*

Not because your doing anything wrong.

Parents go behind closed doors to have physical relations.

They also go behind closed doors to be honest and have conflict. And all of this is intimacy. When you are raw and honest with your spouse, that's intimacy.

But it's private. And it should be.

Ever wonder why Moses pitched the Tent of Meeting way, way outside the camp? So people could yell and scream if they needed to. Moses made it clear that the Tent of Meeting was for ANYONE who desired to seek the Lord.

You ever yell and scream at God? No? I wonder if you've experienced true intimacy.

Jesus went way, way off into lonely places. Sometimes he would spend the whole night in prayer.

Principle: Even Jesus needed private times. He needed processing time.

Jesus prayed in front of the disciples. He wasn't afraid to do so. Why would He need to go way off somewhere? What would He need the *whole* night for? Couldn't He say what needed praying in an hour or two?

Jesus needed to say some private things to God. If it weren't private, He wouldn't have needed a lonely place.

He wasn't just talking the whole time. He was processing.

Remember the Garden of Gethsemane? Jesus knew how to process through things with His Father.

Make sure you have a tent of meeting that affords you time to process with God, and privacy to be raw and yell if you need to.

Are you ready for the intimacy you've been missing? God is in the Tent of Meeting. He's waiting to talk to you as a friend.

You just have to come get naked.

Day 29

*"In whom we have boldness and confident **access** through faith in Him." - Ephesians 3:12*

Don't you hate showing up to a restaurant when you're craving that specialty item they offer, only to find they're closed? Or maybe you drive up to Starbucks at 10 p.m., but they locked-up at 9:59?

What's worse is staying in a rural Oklahoma town visiting friends or family. You decide to run to a convenience mart on Sunday afternoon, but no place of business is open. You think, "Who doesn't have a 24-hour convenience store in 2018?!?"

We love having access. It's true, we're a very spoiled and pampered society in America today. But God also created in us a longing for access.

In intimate relationships, access is a key ingredient of health. In a marriage, limited or closed access will starve the relationship. One of Satan's biggest schemes to kill a relationship is convincing one party to put on fig leaves. He does this through shame. He also does this by convincing one party that the other person is holding back.

Moses had the tent of meeting. Anytime He wanted to talk God, outside the camp he'd go. The pillar of cloud would descend and stand at the door. God would talk to him as a friend.

King David said that he'd rather be in the house of the Lord than anywhere else. According to Psalm 63, the lovingkindness David experienced in God's Presence was 'better than life'. It appears David had access to God anytime, just by entering the house of the Lord.

Yet with all this at their disposal, Moses and David would figuratively 'kill' to be in your shoes.

Principle: Moses and King David would trade their access for the access YOU HAVE!

It's true. Moses had as much access to God as Moses could in the Tent of Meeting or on the mount where he met with God. David had as much access as David could have in the tabernacle he made.

BUT YOU HAVE AS MUCH ACCESS TO GOD AS JESUS DOES!

"But God, being rich in mercy, because of His great love with which He loved us, even when we were dead in our transgressions, made us alive together with Christ (by grace you have been saved), and raised us up with Him, and seated us with Him in the heavenly places in Christ Jesus."
-Ephesians 2:4-6

What in the world does it mean that you are 'seated in heavenly places in Christ Jesus'? Are you on a throne in the sky right now? No.
It means just what Paul said in verse 18 of that chapter and in verse 12 of the next: YOU HAVE ACCESS.

Anytime. Anyplace. Anywhere.

"Therefore, let us draw near with confidence to the throne of grace, so that we may receive mercy and find grace to help in time of need." - Hebrews 4:12

You're never imposing. He's always available.
You don't have to be sinless to have access. You don't have to get your heart right. You don't have to serve more. You don't have to have your emotions settled.

You're already seated there right now if you've been born again.

You only have to do one thing, illustrated several ways:

Lay down.

Expect. (seek, hope, wait)

Walk in the light.

Rest.

Get naked.

Play YOUR role.

Day 30

"And now you know...the rest of the story."
  - Paul Harvey

No one could tell a story quite like Paul Harvey. He was the master of the surprise ending.

I hope this book has already blessed you in some way. But you might be wondering the rest of the story.

"Josh, we've heard what your times with the Lord were like before. What are they like now?"

Great question. In short, TOTALLY DIFFERENT.

I never question if He's there.

I remember feeling I had to do something to get His Presence to come. I never do that anymore. I can sense Him always. Sure, there are differing degrees. There are times of greater visitation and excitement. Isn't that how any relationship is?

I let Him lead.

Many times, I get alone and just lie down. Literally. But every time, I at least sit down and wait. I spend much more time listening than talking.

We pick up where we left off.

Ever go to dinner with a friend and feel like you need to fill them in on all that's happened since you last spoke?

I totally felt this way with God. I felt I had to cover all the ground I might've missed.

I also felt like I was entering the throne room of the King and then exiting into the rest of my day. The next morning, I'd have to start my approach completely over.

Not anymore. We pick up where we left off.

I hear Him so clearly.

But that's not the only cool part. I also don't get worried if I don't hear Him. I figure it's His job to speak. I simply lie down.

I'm not spiritually codependent anymore.

I used to be so worried I'd miss His voice. I wrung my hands about missing the call He has on my life. I was concerned He'd be mad at me or that'd I'd make a mistake.

Now? I figure He'll show me what I need to know. I don't worry about any of those things. It's totally His job.

I get raw and honest with God, telling Him what I really feel.

Not much more to say about that. It's what I do.

I've seen exponentially more answers to prayer.

It's been more than five years since the computer lab experience. I've had more prayers answered in that time than in the previous 35 years combined. One year, we kept track of answered prayers by writing them down on little paper strips and putting them in a jar (Not sure why we stopped.) The jar is overflowing.

WAY more answered prayer. And I probably use 90% fewer words when I pray.

I don't watch the clock.

I was SO into earning and didn't even realize it. I always made sure to spend an hour with God. I don't even watch the clock anymore. Sometimes, hours go by. Some days, I don't have a devotion. Yep, you heard me right. And God is totally OK with it.

I don't feel like there's a certain 'tent of meeting.'

May seem weird to some, but I always felt like I had to have a consecrated place to pray. Not anymore.

Don't get me wrong, some places are just more conducive to prayer than others. And I totally believe I can tell when I'm in a spot where God has often been invited (church sanctuaries, believers' homes, etc.) But I don't stress over the place.

Fruit just grows.

I stopped trying to not sin. OH, THE FREEDOM! Not freedom to run and sin! Heavens no! Freedom from the yoke of slavery.

Self-control just grows. I started eating healthier. Just because I suddenly wanted to. I found a system that works. Doesn't mean there weren't challenges. Lost 23 pounds and feel great.

I have the fruit of joy, love, and peace. They just spring up. I don't have to work them up, or 'get my praise on.'

Anxiety continues to decline. The peace I feel is

indescribable.

I list this here because revelation about how to let God spend time with me helped tremendously. However, I encourage those struggling with anxiety or depression to go see a good, Jesus-loving therapist. Pastors are awesome, but 99% aren't equipped to deal with depression, anxiety, addictions, etc. It's ok. God has them serving a different purpose.

The Lord gave us therapists. Go see one!

I truly would rather be in my devotion than anywhere.

Truly. It's better than anything. Hands down.

Made in the USA
Columbia, SC
28 November 2018